T0265700

Quilts from the Country

This book is dedicated to the memory of my beloved Dad, Rex...
who opened my eyes to the beauty in nature and showed me
the glory of the countryside in all its forms.

I am closest to you in the country.

STUART HILLARD

Quilts from the Country

Seasonal patchwork projects for your home

PAVILION

Contents

Quilting all year round

I made my first full-sized bed quilt thirty years ago.
It was a country-style 'Trip Around the World' quilt,
made up of simple squares in a pattern of concentric
diamonds using florals, stripes and gingham fabrics.
I was living in a large city at the time, just out of
university. I longed to be back home in the countryside,
surrounded by nature and the things I had grown up
with. I spent many evenings after work stitching the
squares together: a little rosebud print one night, a
plaid in shades of forest green another. The piece
took shape and eventually was quilted and bound.
Throughout the making I had felt the peace and
tranquility of home and I felt that even more strongly
once the quilt was finished and placed on my bed. My
love affair with quilting had begun, and my love has
only deepened over time!

Why *country-style* quilts?

I grew up in Tewkesbury, Gloucestershire, and thanks
to my father fell in love with the little things that make
it such a magical place to live. He taught me about the
flora and fauna around us, and the people who relied
on the land and the way that the seasons changed
things. We walked through bright golden cornfields
in summer and marvelled at the colours; collected
fallen leaves and twigs of bright, jewel-like berries in
autumn; bagged pocketfuls of snagged lambswool on
fences in spring; and sheltered in the woods on winter
days to watch the snowflakes fall. Dad shared with
me his love of simple things and of times past – these
things feed my soul now as they did then.

There are so many reasons to love country-style quilts;
the style and colours are inextricably linked to the rural
landscape, to the sky and the sea. They are also linked
to the animals, birds and people who live there, and to
the turning tide of seasons. I suppose at their heart is
something reassuringly familiar, as if they came from
grandma's attic. Country-style quilts take us to another
place and time that was simpler and more peaceful
– and not just when they are finished and being used
and loved, but during the making too. If you love the
traditions of quilting, and the home, family, comfort
and warmth that quilting represents, I know you'll love
spending the year with me, quilting in the country.

What makes a quilt?

A quilt is generally accepted to be a softly padded thin bedcovering consisting of three layers: a quilt top, a backing fabric and a warm padded layer in the middle. The three layers are held together with some form of stitching or ties and the edges are neatly bound. The word quilt comes from the Latin *culcita* meaning 'stuffed sack' – a bolster perhaps, or a cushion. Quilting was originally brought to Europe in the twelfth or thirteenth century from the Middle East, and in its early incarnation was made into protective clothing, worn under armour. Quilted bed hangings, window coverings, clothing and bed quilts are found in almost every culture around the globe – the desire for warmth and protection is universal and so is the quilt!

The top This is where the action happens. The top can be patchwork, made up of small patches of scraps sewn together; a larger, more cohesive design; individual 'blocks' joined in neat rows; or a large central 'medallion' surrounded by frames. A quilt can be appliquéd and decorated with patches stitched onto a background, or a combination of the two. Quilt tops are sometimes 'wholecloth', where the beauty comes from a single fabric or the quilting stitches themselves. While many quilt tops from the past were hand stitched, most are now machine sewn but they carry the love, skill and meaning of their past selves.

The middle This is what I like to think of as the business end of a quilt. It's the bit you never see, and probably never think of either, but it's the layer that provides warmth and protection. The middle section of a quilt is called 'wadding' or 'batting' and nowadays is most likely to be made of cotton or polyester or a combination of the two. In times past, this layer was more likely to be made from carded sheep's wool, laid out in a thin layer to trap heat and wick moisture from the body. In leaner times, rags, old clothing or blankets, or even a worn-out older quilt, might provide this essential middle layer.

The back This is the underside of the quilt and just like the middle is often out of sight and out of mind. It plays just as important a role as the top and middle. The backing of a quilt can be, and usually is 'wholecloth' but it can be made of strips of fabric decoratively sewn together, panels, squares or even a completely different design to the top. The back of a quilt is something the recipient and user will see lots of, so make it beautiful!

Let's not forget the quilting stitches! The quilting stitches penetrate all three layers and hold the whole thing together. Whether done by hand or machine, they can be utilitarian and hardly visible or really enhance and complement your patchwork or appliqué design. Either way, they are an integral part of your quilt.

Useful equipment:
the hard stuff

If you're already a quilter then you will almost certainly have most of what you'll need to start your country quilting adventure. If this is your first foray into patchwork, then you are in for a treat! You will need some basic equipment. Don't be put off by the list, these things can last a lifetime.

Sewing machine

You'll need a sewing machine that sews a good straight stitch and, for the majority of quiltmaking, it needn't be more complex than that. A zigzag stitch and a blanket stitch are useful both for machine appliqué and dressmaking. You'll need a ¼" (6mm) foot for your machine. Most patchwork relies on an accurate ¼" (6mm) seam allowance and these feet are available for most machines. If you're doing a lot of paper foundation piecing it is useful to have an open-toed foot to allow good visibility when you are stitching. It's useful to have a zipper foot for attaching covered piping cord and trim to cushions, a 'darning' or 'free motion' foot, and a 'walking foot' for machine quilting. These are usually optional extras, but well worth having.

Scissors

I like a large pair of shears for cutting fabric, and small pointed embroidery scissors for cutting out appliqués and finer details. It's also worth having a pair of 'paper only' scissors for cutting out paper templates and foundations as using your fabric scissors on paper will blunt them.

Thread snips ②

Because nothing dulls scissors' blades like snipping thread.

Pins ③

I like fine long pins for piecing and shorter fine pins for appliqué. Lace, lingerie or bridal pins are most suitable; buy quality pins, and don't sew over them!

Hand sewing needles

I like milliners' needles or sharps for hand appliqué and hand sewing the quilt binding. For hand embroidery I use a crewel or embroidery needle. For quilting I use a 'between' needle. The most economical way of buying these is in multipacks containing different sizes.

Machine needles

I love Microtex needles for my machine piecing, appliqué and quilting and generally use a 70 or 75 for everything if I can get away with it. The lower the number, the finer the needle, so these are quite fine. They are wonderful for precision piecing and the almost invisible machine appliqué. The only downside is they cannot be used with your sewing machine's automatic needle threader, so get yourself a hand needle threader or a magnifying glass! Use a larger needle if you are having problems with threads breaking, and of course match your needle to your thread type, particularly if you use embroidery or metallic threads. Change your needles regularly; I recommend after 6–8 hours of sewing time, or before if you notice skipped or poorly formed stitches or the needle gets bent. I know that sounds very frequent, but think of machine needles like disposable razors – a blunt razor looks fine until you try shaving with it.

Wooden embroidery hoops

These double hoops are placed under and over a piece of fabric to hold it taut while you are working hand embroidery. Choose a size that is smaller than the piece of fabric being worked on. A larger diameter will give you a clearer view of your work and a bigger working area. Don't leave fabric in a hoop when you are not working on the piece, or the fabric may become permanently distorted. A 4-6 in hoop is a useful size

Rotary cutter, ruler and self-healing mat

The holy trinity of cutting! Always use these three items together for accuracy and safety. I like a trigger grip cutter, a 6" x 24" (15.2 x 61cm) perspex ruler and an A2 self-healing cutting mat as my basic kit.

Other rulers

A 12" (30.5cm) or 15" (38.1cm) square is wonderful for cutting larger pieces and for trimming quilts after quilting. I love a smaller ruler, say 6" x 12" (15.2 x 30.5cm), and a mat for cutting scraps and smaller projects. I also love my 4½" (11.4cm) and 6½" (16.5cm) 'square up' rulers, which are brilliant for cutting units such as half square triangles (HSTs) and quarter square triangles (QSTs), and flying geese units (see page 30). I have recently fallen in love with the Creative Grids Non-Slip 6" (15.2cm) Flying Geese and 45 Degree and 90 Degree Triangle Ruler. It is heaven sent for creating HST, QST and flying geese units quickly, easily and accurately.

Template plastic, dressmaker's tissue paper and freezer paper

These items are perfect for cutting templates for curved shapes, appliqués, pattern pieces and for those who prefer to cut with scissors. I have all three in my stash because they all have their own uses. Cereal box cardboard is another option, particularly if only a few shapes are required. Freezer paper is an American product, used to wrap meat before putting in the freezer. It has a matt side and a shiny waxy side. I particularly like using freezer paper, available in the UK from quilt shops and from online retailers, for templates as I'm a bit clumsy and freezer paper will 'stick' to the fabric with the heat of an iron and then won't slip while you cut out. It peels off without leaving a residue and can be reused a number of times.

Bias tape makers

These clever little gadgets allow us to make very neat folded strips of fabric perfect for appliqué (stems for example) or for binding quilt edges or seams in dressmaking. I like the ⅜" (1cm) for appliqué and 1" (2.5cm) for binding seams, but a variety of sizes is available.

Spray starch

Spray starch is an absolute must for quilters. I use it all the time to prepare fabric for cutting. Spray, wait a moment or two and then iron to create crisp, flat fabric that cuts cleanly and pieces easily without distortion. If you prefer a starch-free alternative, look for Mary Ellen's Best Press.

Fabric marking pens and pencils

It's useful to have fabric-safe marking pencils or pens in your kit. Sometimes a regular propelling pencil, which is thin and remains consistent, is all you need to mark a diagonal line for stitching on the wrong side of a HST. You might need to mark embroidery lines, in which case an air- or water-erasable pen is better. You might try a chalk pencil for marking quilting lines or a crafting pen, erasable with the heat of an iron. Always test your pen or pencil on scrap fabric before committing. There is no single perfect marking pen – it's good to have a selection for different uses.

Curved safety pins

Ideal for pinning the layers of a quilt together in preparation for quilting. Buy in bulk as you will need hundreds to pin-baste a large quilt.

Adhesive spray

A spray glue (I like Odif 505 Temporary Adhesive) is used to hold the layers of a quilt together temporarily, eliminating the need for pinning or traditional thread basting (tacking). Always use in a well-ventilated room or outdoors and away from pets. Don't be tempted to substitute fabric adhesive spray for spray mount, which are not the same thing and may damage your quilt and/or sewing machine.

Useful equipment: *the soft stuff*

This is the stuff that we stitchers and quilters really get excited about! For my quilting projects I generally use 100% cotton, quilt-weight fabric. Cotton washes really well, is easy to cut, sew and press and comes in the most incredible array of colours and patterns. Good-quality quilting cottons are generally very reliable, have minimal shrinkage and are unlikely to 'bleed' colour when washed. I sometimes use cotton-linen mix fabrics, which have slightly more texture than 100 per cent cotton and make lovely backgrounds for country-style projects. Keep an eye out for 'natural seeded calico or cotton', which also has an 'old-time' look that would suit many of the projects in this book. Cotton lawn is also very suitable for quilting. The best known is Tana Lawn made by Liberty Fabrics and, although a little lighter than regular quilt-weight cotton, it can be mixed in very successfully.

When I shop for fabrics I often go with a plan. The plan is not always stuck to, but when I do I tend to look for fabrics around a theme or a colour. I like to buy fabrics 'off the bolt' in either ½ or 1 metre pieces and if I really like something I'll buy 3 or 4 metres, particularly if it will work well as sashings (see page 38) or a border. Sometimes I'll just see what pops out at me. It might be a selection of creams, tans and neutral background prints, which might work in any number of projects and are so worthwhile having in your stash. I'll generally buy ½ metre cuts, especially if I find eight or ten that I like!

There are a great many kinds of quilting fabrics out there and I love them all! Woven and printed stripes, plains (or 'solids' as they are often called), chambrays, polka dots, plaids, prints and batiks – the choice can be mind-boggling and it can seem overwhelming if you're a newbie. Quilters' 'pre-cuts' can really help in this situation!

What's a pre-cut?

As the name suggests, these are ready-cut pieces of fabric, usually available in bundles or sets and created with quilters in mind. Originally cut and bundled by quilt store owners, they are now manufactured by fabric companies too, often with whole fabric ranges available in a very tempting package. Pre-cuts are brilliant for trying out new designs, expanding your comfort zone and encouraging you to use designs, patterns and colours that you might otherwise avoid.

Fat quarters

The original pre-cut was the 'fat quarter', an 18" x 21" (45.7 x 53cm) piece of fabric. This comes from a ½ metre of fabric that has been split down the middle, and is a useful size and shape for quilting. A good stock of fat quarters is useful in any quilter's stash and many quilt shops sell coordinating packs, which can be a great starting point for a project.

Fat eighths

These smaller cuts are half of a fat quarter, or approximately 9" x 21" (22.9 x 53cm). They are often sold in coordinating bundles and offer great variety for a minimal spend.

Charm packs

A charm square is a 5" x 5" (12.7 x 12.7cm) square of pre-cut fabric, often with a pinked or zigzag edge. A charm pack is a collection of coordinating charm squares, often created by fabric manufacturers to allow the quilter to own an entire fabric collection for a minimal spend. Charm packs tend to contain 40–42 squares in a variety of prints, often with some repeats. They are a great way to collect lots of variety, but keep in mind that the fabric quantities of each are very small.

Layer cakes

These larger squares, at 10" (25.4cm), are ideal if you love the variety of a 5" (12.7cm) charm pack but need bigger pieces of fabric. They are my favourite way to build my stash, particularly when I need to a solid base that I can then supplement with scraps. Layer Cakes (made by Moda Fabrics) or 10" (25.4cm) charm packs are usually built from one designer or range and will coordinate beautifully. Larger squares are also a great source of fabric for appliqué, when you need lots of colours and shades. They can be found in solids and watercolour batiks – perfect for creating appliqué flowers, stems and leaves.

Jelly roll strips

These are pre-cut and usually taken from one designer's fabric collection. They contain forty–forty-two strips 2½" (6.4cm) wide. Each strip is cut across the width of the fabric, so will be 42–44" (106.7–111.7cm) in length. Jelly roll strips can be very useful for patchwork blocks, especially those made from strips or for sashings (see page 38), bindings and borders.

To pre-wash or not to pre-wash ... that is the question!

Some quilters like to wash their fabrics before they cut them up and use them. If you do this, wash on a low temperature with colour-safe liquid or powder. Wash similar colours together and throw in a handful of colour catchers just in case any of the fabrics run. Don't wash pre-cuts, jelly rolls, charm packs or layer cakes, which are best used straight out the packet.

Wadding or batting – what's in a name?

The terms wadding, batting or 'batt' are interchangeable. It's the stuff that goes inside a quilt to provide the padding and much of the warmth. Most quilters use a cotton or cotton-polyester mix (80/20 is my favourite) but there are alternatives such as bamboo, wool and pure polyester. Cotton battings are perfect for the home quilter as they are thin and easy to manage under a domestic sewing machine. Battings that contain polyester tend to be a little thicker and

loftier and show off quilting beautifully, but the extra bulk can make them more difficult to handle in larger projects. Wool is a great choice for temperate, damp countries like the UK but is more expensive than cotton and there are fewer options avaliable. Battings come in a wide array of prices, and that can influence many quilters, but keep in mind that this layer can make or break a quilt. Pick a good-quality one whatever material you choose.

Backing fabrics – out of sight, out of mind?

Backing fabric, the essential third layer of a quilt, is often an afterthought, a bit of a grudge purchase and subject to a certain amount of abuse. Worn old sheets, polycotton duvet covers, blankets; they've all found their way onto the back of a quilt and I suppose in an emergency ... nope, I still wouldn't do it! The backing of a quilt needs and deserves to be made of the same great-quality cotton as the front. Some quilters push the boat out and buy more fabrics from the same quilting ranges as the front, piece a backing and make their quilt reversible.

If I'm working on a quilt that is up to 76" (193cm) wide or long, I will piece two widths of regular quilt cotton together with a 1" (2.5cm) seam, pressing the seam open and removing the selvedges. I keep an eye out in quilt shops and online for sale fabrics which work within my favourite colour palettes. I'll buy 3–6 metres for my stash, depending on how much I like it or the price! Solids work perfectly well for backing quilts and are usually less expensive. I may also over-dye fabrics with machine wash dyes to get the colour I want. I sometimes use specially woven 'backing fabrics', which are printed fabrics woven to 108–120" (274.3–304.8cm) wide, so they can be used for really large quilts without the need to piece several widths together. I'll do anything not to have to join backing fabrics, and they are more economical than joining three widths together. Lots of designers now include two or three extra-wide backing fabrics in their ranges, so keep an eye out.

Binding fabrics

I always use regular quilt cotton for the binding, and if I'm making a quilt I'll generally use two ½" (13mm) strips and make double-fold binding (see page 45) because it's strong and lasts well. You can buy ready-made bias binding. I don't as it tends to be pretty low quality and, while it's fine for binding seams inside a garment, it's not meant for the edge of a beautiful handmade heirloom.

Cushion pads

I tend to buy these, also called pillow forms, ready-made unless I need a very specific size and shape. I like feather pads for my cushions or pillows and I buy either the exact size or one or two inches larger for a really plump look. If you prefer hypoallergenic fibrefill, opt for the correct size for your project, as polyester filling gives a much fuller look.

Toy stuffing

For projects such as my Crazy Scrap Hanging Hearts (see page 117) and Embroidered Tree Decorations (see page 199), use toy stuffing. It comes in small or large bags and is usually hypoallergenic and machine washable. For an eco-friendly alternative, use scraps of fabric, thread waste and scraps of quilt batting, finely chopped up with scissors or using a rotary cutter and mat.

Fusible web

Fusible web is available from a variety of manufacturers and in several different weights including a heavyweight which does not need sewing at all. The most readily available brand is called Bondaweb which specialises in a paper-backed fusible webbing, which is used to create raw edge machine appliqué. When you're using paper-backed webbing, it's helpful to scratch a small X on the back of the paper with a pin and then peel the paper out from this cross. This stops you fraying the edges of your shape.

Interfacing

Interfacing adds an extra layer to fabric, sometimes to make the fabric stiffer, as in a collar or pockets, or to stop the fabric stretching out of shape or distorting, for example when adding embroidery to a quilted project. I use lightweight interfacing to create 'faced' appliqué (see page 36).

It's really useful to have in your stash. I use a medium or lightweight interfacing and I switch between woven and non-woven versions – either is suitable for the projects in this book. Interfacing is easy to find online or in haberdashery departments.

Thread

I always keep in mind that thread is the very stuff that holds my whole project together. Often the unsung hero of a project, thread is one of those things that's worth spending a little more on. The better the thread, the better the light fastness, durability and strength – it's all good!

Thread for piecing

I use a 'sew-all' polyester for the majority of my piecing. For precise and accurate patchwork, use 80 weight thread, which is very fine, and a number 70 Microtex needle. The finer the thread, the sharper the piecing! Colour-wise I do most of my piecing with a light tan or grubby greige. These are not glamorous colours, but they do blend with almost everything.

Thread for appliqué

Again, I use a polyester sew-all thread or a pure cotton thread. I like toning colours, but I don't get too hung up on exact matches. Once your thread is sewn down, a near match is usually perfect in practice. You could also try sewing all your appliqués pieces with a black or dark grey thread and a machine blanket stitch for a gorgeous folk art look.

Thread for quilting

Sew-all thread can be used for quilting and I often do very successfully. If you have the perfect colour in regular thread, why not use it? Special quilting threads are also available. They are often a little bit thicker, and come in all sorts of gorgeous colours including multicolours and variegated versions. If you're using a thicker thread make sure you use a thicker needle made for quilting. These needles have longer, sharper points designed to pierce through your quilt cleanly, creating perfectly formed stitches. I longarm quilt (see page 44) most of my work and I use Glide Trilobal polyester thread, which has a fabulous light sheen and is really beautiful for quilting. There are lots lots of beautiful colours and it's suitable for domestic quilting too.

Thread for embroidery

Sometimes called 'floss', this is the stuff that comes in skeins or hanks and is generally six threads twisted together. This thread is designed for hand sewing. For most projects, use two threads at a time. For a bolder line or outline, possibly use three. Make sure you use a crewel or embroidery needle. Embroidery floss comes in a huge variety of solid colours as well as lovely variegated and multicolour threads. As always, go for quality every time.

Basic techniques

Rotary cutting

For the majority of my quiltmaking I use the rotary cutting system and, when you know how, it's accurate, fast and easy to do. You'll need what I like to call 'The Holy Trinity of Quilting' which, unsurprisingly, consists of three very important pieces of equipment.

Rotary cutter

This is a circular blade mounted on a handle. As you push away the blade rotates and cuts through up to eight layers of fabric. Beginners should start by cutting one layer at a time and building up to more. My own limit is four layers; beyond that I get ruler slippage. The most useful size cutter to buy is one with a 45mm blade. For speedy cutting of long strips and borders I switch to my 60mm cutter, and for cutting curves and around templates I like a 28mm cutter.

Rotary cutting ruler

A rotary cutting ruler is an ⅛" (3mm) thick perspex ruler made to use with a rotary cutter, marked in a grid of inches with smaller increments (they are also available with centimetre markings). Most also have lines showing the 45 and 60 degree angles. Use the ruler to measure and cut your fabric. The most useful size to buy is a 6" x 24" (15.2 x 61cm), although I also like a 6" x 12" (15.2 x 30.5cm) for smaller fabric pieces and a couple of square up rulers at 4½" (11.4cm) and 6½" (16.5cm).

Do not substitute any other kind of ruler – you must use one designed specifically for rotary cutters! You can also buy speciality rulers and acrylic templates designed to be used with a rotary cutting mat and cutter. If the quilt you're making has a very specific shape that's repeated a lot, it might be a real time-saver.

Self-healing mat

This goes on your work surface with the fabric and ruler on top, then you cut. The mat protects your table from the blade and has grid lines printed on it to help you measure and square up the fabric. The most useful size to buy is 18" x 24" (45.7 x 61cm), which is slightly bigger than A2. I also like a smaller A4-sized mat for trimming, squaring up small units and turning scraps of fabric into usable patches.

Fabric prep

Get the iron out and press those fabrics. Even fabric that has come straight off the bolt needs pressing, and scraps that have been lingering in a pile will definitely need straightening. Press well, using steam. I like to use a cotton setting, lots of steam and some spray starch (see page 14), which will help to tighten the weave, minimise shrinkage and get everything nice and flat ready for cutting and piecing. The spray starch will make the fabric a little firmer and stiffer and will reduce the amount it can stretch. This really helps if you're a less experienced quilter or you are working with fabric cut on the bias, as the crisper fabric is easier to piece.

Straightening fabric edges

Start by straightening the edge of your fabric. Fold it, selvedge to selvedge, and place on your mat with the fold at the bottom. Position the straight line on your ruler on the fold and hold the ruler firmly down with your left hand (do the reverse if you are left-handed). Stick out your little (pinky) finger and place on the mat to help steady your hand. Push the blade of your rotary cutter out, position it against the ruler about 1" (2.5cm) below the start of your fabric on the right-hand side and push the blade firmly up the edge of the ruler. Once you have cut about 6" (15.2cm) of fabric, stop cutting and move your left hand up the ruler before continuing, to prevent the ruler slipping.

Cutting strips

Give the mat a half turn so that the straightened edge is on the left and the fold is at the top. Do this in preference to turning the fabric. You've just cut a perfectly straight edge and turning the fabric will disturb that straight edge. Position your ruler on top of the fabric with the top of the ruler lined up with the fold and the width of strip you require under the ruler. Use the grid lines on the ruler to measure the strip width; the fabric to the right of the ruler that is not covered is spare. Position the cutter at the bottom of the ruler with the blade out and push it along the ruler edge. If you require more strips, simply move the ruler over to the right by the required width and cut again. If the strip you require is wider than your ruler, turn your ruler on its side – you now have 24" (61cm) of ruler to work with instead of 6" (15.2cm). Cut about 5" (12.7cm), then move the ruler along and continue to cut.

Cutting rectangles, squares and triangles

Cut strips to the required width, then cut those strips into rectangles or squares. To make triangles, cut rectangles or squares on the diagonal.

Try this handy exercise to see if you're sewing an accurate ¼" (6mm) seam

Cut three pieces of fabric, each 2½ x 4½" (6.4 x 11.4cm). Using your ¼" (6mm) foot, sew two of the strips together then press the seam one way. Now add the last rectangle to the top. It should fit perfectly ... but does it?

If the last strip is too long, your seam allowance is too big and needs slimming down. If the last strip is too small, then your seam allowance is a bit on the skinny side and needs fattening up a bit. It's easy to make these small adjustments now before you start on a project.

If you don't have a ¼" (6mm) foot for your machine but you are able to move your needle position, you can use the regular foot on your sewing machine to sew a perfect ¼" (6mm) seam allowance. You need to move your needle position over to the right a bit – this is usually done by adjusting the stitch width while in straight stitch mode. Place your rotary cutting ruler under the foot of your machine with the edge of the ruler aligned with the edge of your presser foot. Keep moving the needle position using the stitch width adjustment and hand cranking the needle down to touch the ruler until it is just on the ¼" (6mm) mark. Take a note of the needle position for future reference.

If you can't move the needle, then place your ruler as before so that the needle just touches the ¼" (6mm) mark, then place a strip of masking tape onto the bed of your sewing machine. Use this tape as a guide for your fabric.

Check your ¼" (6mm) seam allowance regularly! I like to make a unit for a block, for example a four-patch, then measure it and check that this unit is the correct size for the block I am making. Then I make one entire block and measure it. It's much better to know that adjustments are needed now, before you make the remaining 99 blocks!

Whether you use imperial (inch) or metric (centimetre) measurements, stick to one system – don't mix the two!

Cutting patches from irregular scraps

You can cut squares, rectangles and all kinds of other patches from your irregular leftover pieces. First determine the 'straight of grain' to ensure that your cut fabric is as stable as it can be. This is easy on a full width of fabric, as the grain (the direction of the woven threads) runs parallel to the selvedge. On a small scrap you'll need to look closer. You want the weave of the fabric to be as straight as possible when you make that first cut. Straighten one edge, keeping the straight edge 'on-grain', and then use that cut edge to line up your ruler for the second, third and subsequent cuts.

Using templates

Some shapes can't be cut easily using a rotary cutter and ruler; curves, circles and other odd shapes require a slightly different approach. You can draw and cut templates for many simple shapes, and this is particularly useful if you only have scissors.

My favourite template material is freezer paper (see page 14). Trace the desired shape carefully onto the matt side. Use a ruler for straight edges and make sure the template you are tracing has the ¼" (6mm) seam allowance added. (All the piecing templates in this book do, but appliqué shapes are always shown without a seam allowance.) Cut the paper template out carefully with scissors.

If you only have a few shapes to cut then simply iron on the freezer paper, shiny side against the fabric, then cut out the shape. The paper will peel off when you've finished cutting out and can be reused a number of times. If you need to cut out a large number of one shape, it's worth ironing your freezer paper to thin card to make a more durable template. If you use template plastic (see page 14) Keep it away from your iron ... it melts!'

It's also possible to buy acrylic templates in many commonly used shapes such as triangles, squares, hexagons, half hexagons and clamshells. These acrylic shapes can be placed on top of multiple layers of fabric and rotary-cut around. This will speed up the process considerably.

Piecing your patchwork

Patchwork is sewn with a ¼" (6mm) seam and if everything is going to fit together perfectly, accuracy really matters. You may have a ¼" (6mm) or 'patchwork' foot for your sewing machine. These are handy but they don't guarantee accuracy – only you can control that.

Sewing patchwork pieces

1   Place fabrics right sides together.

2   Match the ends first and pin well.

3   Sew the seam using a stitch length of 2.2–2.6.

4   Clip threads as you go.

5   Press seams one way, usually towards the darker fabric to avoid 'show through'. Alternatively, press your seams open to distribute the bulk evenly. I particularly like doing this when I'm sewing smaller patchwork, have lots of seams converging or I'm in any doubt about which way to press. Pressing open is my choice more and more these days.

Strip piecing

This can really speed up the process of patchwork, particularly when sewing units with squares and rectangles. You sew strips of fabric together and then cut segments from the resulting panel.

1   Place two strips right sides together and pin.

2   Sew the seam using a slightly shorter than normal stitch length. A stitch length of 2 is perfect.

3   Press the seam one way.

4   Continue to add strips and press until your strip pieced panel is the desired size.

5   Cross-cut your panel into suitably sized segments.

Basic patchwork units

These are a few basic patchwork units that crop up all the time. Here are my favourite methods to produce these quickly and accurately.

Half square triangle (HST)

To calculate the size of fabric you need to cut for this method, start with the finished size you require. For example, for a 3" (7.6cm) square finished size, add ⅞" (2.2cm) and cut two 3⅞" (9.8cm) squares – often one light fabric and one dark. To make a pair of matching HSTs, proceed as follows.

1 Pair the two squares with right sides together and mark the diagonal on one of them with a fine mechanical pencil. Ensure your line is drawn accurately from corner to corner.

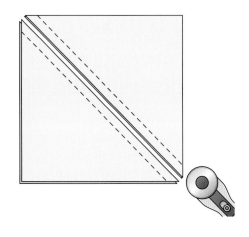

4 Trim the 'dog ears' neatly as shown.

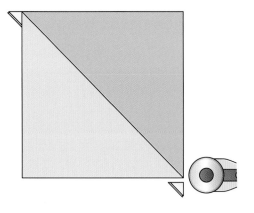

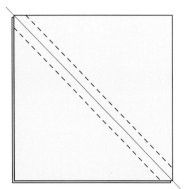

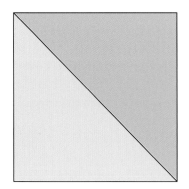

2 Sew a ¼" (6mm) either side of the drawn line.

3 Cut along the drawn line. Open up the two HSTs and press each of the seams one way.

Sewing triangles

If you want to mix your fabrics up more, you can cut each square in half on the diagonal to produce triangles, switch them around and then sew together with a ¼" (6mm) seam. Be careful as you sew, as cutting on the diagonal exposes the bias edge, which is easy to stretch out of shape. I use this method more and more these days. I find it so much quicker to pair up my fabrics in long strips, cut triangle pairs and then seam them – it's amazing how much time I save by not marking that centre line!

Making larger and trimming back

Lots of quilters like to make their HSTs larger than they need and then trim them to size. Although it's an extra process, it does almost guarantee patchwork perfection! Many quilters find the odd (⅞") measurement hard to cut. Add ⅛" (3mm) – or 1" (2.5cm) in total, to the size of the squares or triangles needed to make the number whole and therefore easier to measure and cut. If the pattern calls for two and ⅞" (2.2cm) squares cross-cut on the diagonal to yield two HSTs, add ⅛" (3mm). So cut 3" (7.6cm) instead. Piece your HST units then trim to 2½ x 2½" (6.4 x 6.4cm). When you trim HSTs make sure that you use a small square ruler and align the 45 degree line with the pieced diagonal, corner to corner. Trim a sliver off each side to make the unit the correct unfinished size for your pattern.

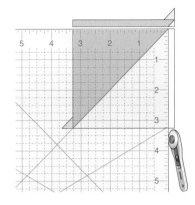

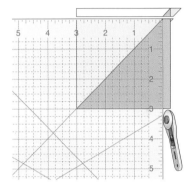

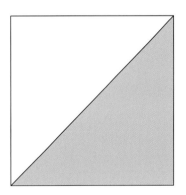

Quarter square triangle (QST) or hourglass units

To calculate the size of fabric you need to cut to make QSTs, start with the finished size required. For example, for 3" (7.6cm) finished size, add 1¼" (3.2cm) and cut two squares to 4¼" (10.8cm). Proceed as follows.

1   Pair two squares, right sides together, usually one light and one dark. Mark both diagonals with a pencil.

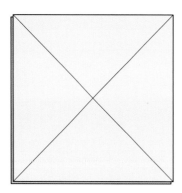

2   Sew ¼" (6mm) from the pencil line on the same side of each quarter triangle as shown.

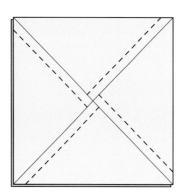

3   Cut along the drawn lines.

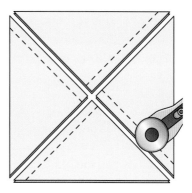

4   Open up the pieces and press seams one way.

5   Sew together pairs of units to yield two QSTs.

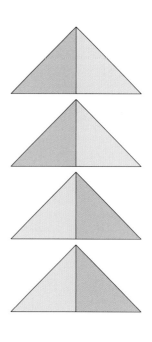

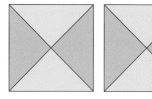

Stitch and flip

This is a great method for adding triangles to larger blocks and is sometimes referred to as 'snowballing'. It is also a very accurate method for making Square in a Square units (see page 33).

1   Take one small square (this will become the triangle corner) and lightly mark the diagonal in pencil on the wrong side. Place this small square on top of the patch you wish to 'snowball', right sides together, with the diagonal line running across the corner. Pin in place.

2   Stitch on the marked diagonal line (or even a thread's width inside the line). Flip the corner back and press. If the flipped square lines up exactly with the background, all is well and you can flip it back, trim the underside away and press again. If the results aren't as accurate as you'd like, unpick, have another go and check again.

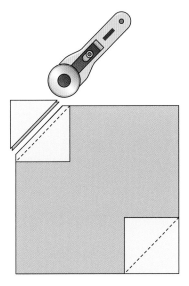

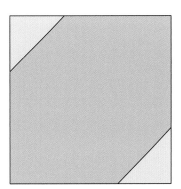

Flying geese unit

This is the 'no waste' method. To calculate the size of fabric you need to cut for flying geese units start with the finished size. Flying geese are generally twice as long as they are high. The example below makes a sample of four flying geese units, 6 x 3" (15.2 x 7.6cm). One fabric represents the 'geese' and the other the 'sky'.

Fabric A (geese): add one ¼" (3.2cm) to the finished length of the unit, making 7¼" (18.4cm). Cut one square for four units.

Fabric B (sky): finished height of unit + ⅞" (2.2cm) square, making 3⅞" (9.8cm). Cut four squares for four units.

1 Cut one square of fabric A and four squares of fabric B.

2 Place two of the smaller squares on top of the larger square, right sides together as shown. The small squares will overlap slightly in the centre.

3 Mark the diagonal through the centre of the small squares lightly with a pencil.

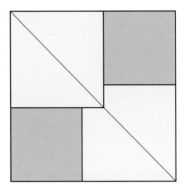

4 Sew ¼" (6mm) either side of the drawn line and then cut along the drawn line.

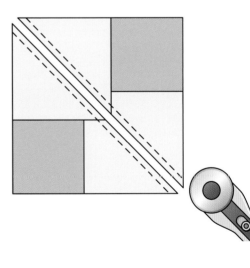

5 Working on one of the halves, flip back the two small square halves and press.

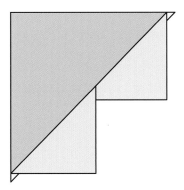

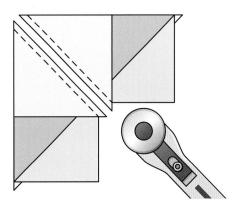

7 Repeat with the remaining pieced half created in step 4.

6 Add another small square, right sides together as shown. Mark the diagonal on the back of the small square, then sew ¼" (6mm) either side of this marked line. Cut apart on the drawn line. Flip the triangles back and press.

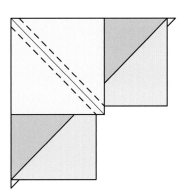

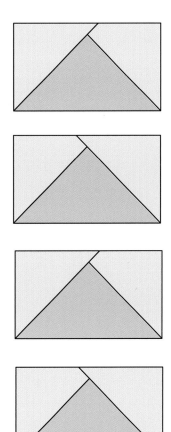

Precise piecing

Whether sewing four patches or an elaborately pieced block, we all want our work to be beautiful and the process to be fun. Follow my top tips for patchwork perfection!

1   Prep your fabrics with starch and steam.

2   Cut your patches and strips as accurately as possible.

3   Test and check your ¼" (6mm) seam allowance. Don't just measure your seam – sew units together and check the sewn measurements. Adjust your needle position if needed to get the most accurate seam allowance.

4   Use fine thread for piecing and a fine needle, changing your needle regularly.

5   Press, don't iron. Once the seam is sewn, set your seam by running an iron along the seam in the direction you sewed it. Flip the fabrics open or to one side and press from the front. Make sure the fabric lies absolutely flat and isn't folded or pleated.

6   Make one set of units and one test block first, and check your measurements at every step. If they are not the correct size, adjust your cutting, sewing or pressing as needed. Identify the problem at this stage; don't save it up for later.

7   Embrace the unpicker! If you're not happy with a seam, unpick it and have another go. It only takes a few minutes and it's worth the effort.

8   Use pins, even for small units. Match the ends, any match points and then at regular spaces in between. Take your pins out before you get to them!

9   Use a light touch when handling your patchwork. When you are piecing or pressing fabric it is easy to stretch, distort and generally mangle it, so treat fabric gently.

10 Remember the big picture. An individual unit might be slightly 'off' and irritating when looked at in isolation, but in the context of a big quilt, will it matter? Choose your battles and remember we are all striving towards our best work!

Paper foundation piecing

Paper foundation is one of my favourite patchwork techniques and once you try it, I'm sure it will become one of yours too. What is paper foundation piecing? It involves machine sewing fabric directly to a sheet of paper that is printed with the patchwork block pattern. Fabric is placed under the pattern and you sew on the printed side, following the lines. It's easy when you know how!

Let's start with an easy block, the Square in a Square.

Print one copy of foundation A, Square in a Square (see below) on regular printer paper. Make sure that you print actual size and measure the printed foundation to check it measures 4½ x 4½" (11.4 x 11.4cm) up to the dashed outer line.

Cutting your fabric patches in advance makes sewing the block much easier. I cut out shapes that are at least ½" (13mm) bigger on all sides than the finished size. Using a rotary cutter means you can cut multiple blocks in one go.

Gather your supplies. You'll need some fairly fine (60wt) cotton or polyester thread in a neutral colour for piecing, an open-

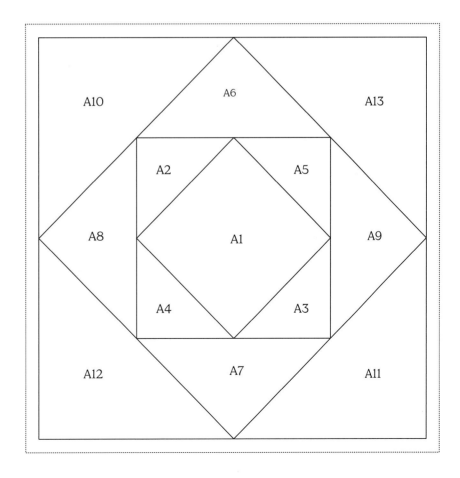

toed foot for your sewing machine, pins and a pair of scissors. You'll also need a piece of card – a postcard is ideal.

Set up your sewing machine. Neutral thread in the top and bobbin, a new needle (size 75 Microtex is my favourite) and set your stitch length to shorter than normal. A stitch length of between 1 and 1.5 is perfect for paper piecing. Next try sewing a piece of paper. The paper should perforate and come apart easily when pulled, but it shouldn't disintegrate as you're sewing.

1   Place your first piece of fabric onto the back of foundation A, right side facing UP. It should cover patch number 1 completely and hang over into the surrounding patches by at least ¼" (6mm). Hold the foundation up to a light source and check! Pin in place.

2   Place patch number 2 on top of patch 1, right side DOWN, raw edges lined up, and pin in place.

3   Turn the foundation over so that the printed side is facing up and sew on the line between patches 1 and 2. Make sure you start and finish sewing at least ¼" (6mm) over the end of the patch.

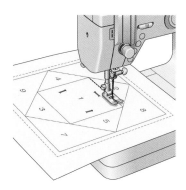

4   Flip the foundation so the fabric is facing you and press patch number 2 back. Hold it up to the light to make sure that is has properly covered number 2 and extends into the surrounding patches by at least ¼" (6mm).

5   Add patches 3, 4 and 5 in the same manner, one at a time, sewing and flipping back and pressing. If your fabric pieces are too big you can trim the excess away. Place the postcard on top of the foundation against the next seamline and fold the paper back against it. This will reveal the overhanging fabric underneath. Place your rotary cutting ruler on top and trim the excess away,

leaving a ¼" (6mm) seam allowance. This makes lining the next patch up very easy!

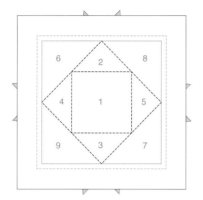

6   Add patches 6, 7, 8 and 9 in the same way.

7   Turn the foundation so the paper side is UP and use a rotary cutter, ruler and mat to trim the block along the outside lines. Be careful here! Use the outer line to trim so that the final ¼" (6mm) seam allowance is included.

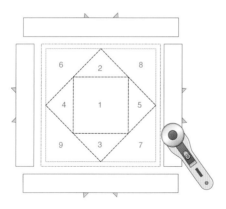

8   Leave the paper intact until all sides of the block have been sewn to something else. Remove the paper by tearing along the sewn lines. The paper should come away very easily but if it doesn't, lightly spritz it with water and leave to soften for 30 seconds. A pair of tweezers is handy for removing tiny pieces of paper left in the seam intersections.

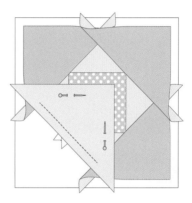

Some blocks require you to make several different foundations (labelled A, B, C and so on). If that's the case, sew the foundations separately then trim the blocks to the outer dashed line (this includes the ¼"/6mm seam allowance). Place foundations A and B, right sides together, then sew on the final printed line. I like to use a very long basting stitch (a stitch length of 5 or 6 on the machine) for doing this. I can then check for correct alignment. If I'm out at all I can easily remove the basting stitches and have another go. If everything is perfect then I re-sew the seam using a very short stitch length (1–1.5).

Appliqué

Appliqué is the process of placing ('applying') one fabric on top of another and sewing it down, and is a perennial favourite of quilters of all persuasions. Appliqué can be 'raw edge' or 'turned edge', and both techniques are easy to learn.

Raw edge or fused appliqué

For this technique you will need a background fabric as well as fabric or fabrics for the appliqués and fusible web (see page 19). Make sure you are using fusible web designed for appliqué (as opposed to fusible interfacing). You'll also need thread to match, or contrast with, your appliqué fabrics.

1   Trace the shape to be appliquéd onto the paper side of the fusible web. Keep in mind that your finished appliqué will be the reverse of your traced image, so letters and numbers, for example, should be reversed for tracing.

2   Roughly cut the shape out of fusible web, leaving approximately ½" (13mm) allowance around your traced image.

3   Fuse the web to the wrong side of your chosen appliqué fabric. It is a good idea to protect the sole plate of your iron from the fusible by covering with baking parchment.

4   When the fabric has cooled, cut the appliqué shape out accurately on your drawn line.

5   Remove the paper backing and lay the appliqué onto your chosen background fabric in its final position.

6   Iron the appliqué shape in place. Use the manufacturer's instructions to guide you to the correct heat setting for your iron.

7   Sew around the edge of your appliqué with matching or contrasting thread to neaten the raw edges and provide more durability. You can use a small zigzag stitch or a blanket stitch to do this.

Turned edge appliqué

Turned edge appliqué is a great choice for quilts that will be used and washed a lot since the raw edges are turned under before stitching. Traditionally this is done by 'needle turning' but this is a slow and laborious process. I have two methods which I prefer to turn the edge.

Faced appliqué

1   Trace the appliqué shape to the smooth side of a piece of lightweight fusible interfacing (the kind used for dressmaking) and cut out roughly.

2   Place the interfacing, glue side to the right side of your chosen appliqué fabric, and sew around the traced shape or along the side that you will turn in step 4. Sew directly on the drawn line. Use a slightly smaller stitch than normal (2 is spot on).

3   Trim the seam to a scant ¼" (6mm) and clip the curves.

4   If you have made a closed shape such as a circle, make a small cut in the back of the interfacing and turn through to the right side. If you have only sewn part of the shape, turn it through the open side.

5   Run the tip of your scissors or a blunt tool such as a chopstick round the edge of the shape and flatten it with your hand. Do not iron it yet.

6   Place the appliqué on your background fabric and iron in place, fusing the glue side of the interfacing to your background fabric. Sew around the shape by hand or machine – no pins required!

Starch and press appliqué

1   Trace the appliqué shape onto thin card – a piece of cereal box is ideal. Cut out neatly, following your drawn line.

2   Cut your chosen appliqué fabric ¼" (6mm) bigger than the card shape on all sides.

3   Paint the ¼" (6mm) of extra fabric with liquid starch. To do this simply spray starch from a can into a small cup and wait until the bubbles settle. Dip a fine paintbrush into the liquid and 'paint' the edges of your appliqué. You want them fully wetted but not dripping!

4   When the entire edge has been turned, remove the card template and re-use.

5   Place the prepared appliqué on your chosen background and pin or baste (tack) it in place. Sew in place by hand or machine.

Sewing the blocks together

Blocks can be sewn straight to other blocks or they can be sewn to plain pieces of fabric the same size as a block (known as alternate blocks). Alternatively, blocks can be sewn to strips or frames – this is known as sashing.

Adding sashings and cornerstones to a quilt

Sashings add a frame around a block and sometimes serve to increase the size of the block and make it 'float'. The blocks are arranged first and then the sashings placed in between them. Sashings are sewn to the top and bottom of alternate blocks and then the vertical columns of blocks and sashings are sewn together. In between these rows are vertical columns of sashings and 'cornerstones', sewn end to end. The cornerstones help to delineate between the rows and columns and are a great way of keeping everything lined up.

Setting a quilt in a 'straight setting'

This simply means that the blocks, or blocks and sashings, are set in vertical and horizontal rows and are pieced as described.

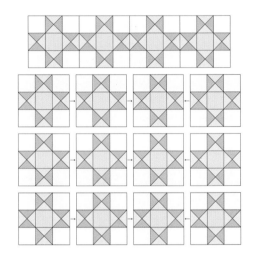

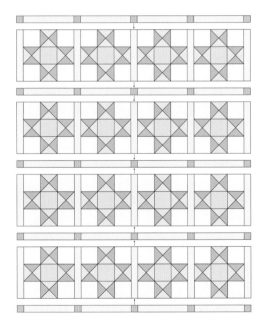

Setting a quilt 'on point'

Here the blocks (and sashings and cornerstones if used) are set in diagonal rows and are pieced as such. Setting blocks in this way leaves a jagged edge that must be filled with 'setting triangles' and 'corner triangles'. Setting triangles are made by cutting large squares on both diagonals to yield QST, and corner triangles are made by cutting large squares on one diagonal to yield HST. The triangles are added to the diagonal rows of blocks and then sewn together in strips.

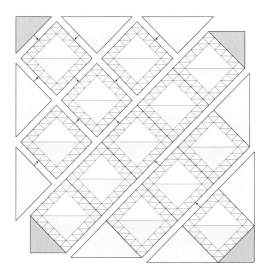

Adding borders to your quilt

Quilts often have one or more borders. Borders can be simple or complex, otherwise known as 'whole' or pieced – the options are endless. Borders can really make a quilt when they are well chosen and well applied. I have added my own choice of borders to many of the quilts in this book but you may wish to customise the pattern. If you are going to do that, try to keep a sense of scale with the quilt centre. A frame around a quilt will draw attention to the centre and usually looks best if the border width is sympathetic to the size of the blocks. For example, if the blocks are 12 inches then a 6-inch border will look better than a 5-inch. You can also make the border 'naturally' fit your quilt by using pieced elements from the blocks.

For example in 'Where the Wind Blows You', I have used flying geese and square on point units from the star blocks to create a natural fit border which perfectly complements their piecing. Follow my tips for border success!

1   Keep a sense of scale. A border is usually there to 'frame' and draw attention to the quilt centre, so keep the proportions of the border sympathetic. Frames that are proportionate to the blocks in the centre look pleasing to the eye so, for example, if the blocks are 10" (25.4cm) then a 5" (12.7cm) border will inevitably look better than a 6" (15.2cm) border. If you're adding multiple borders it's a good idea to keep the total width no bigger than one of the blocks, for example if the blocks are 10" (25.4cm) then you could have 2" (5cm), 6" (15.2cm) and 2" (5cm) borders.

2 Create natural fit borders for your quilt by including elements from the piecing or appliqué in a pieced or appliqué border. Your border will look in proportion and will make sense with the rest of the quilt.

3 Use a multicoloured border fabric to create 'sense' out of a myriad scraps. Quilters often find a patterned border fabric first and choose their colours from this but when we make scrap quilts we inevitably have to work in reverse. Finding a border fabric that is just right can be a challenge so I prefer to pick the border fabric before the blocks are joined together. That way if I need to introduce an extra colour or two to make the border 'work' I can!

4 Add borders to increase the size of a quilt without having to make a huge number of extra blocks. For example, if you want to make a 66 x 72" (168 x 183cm) quilt and you're using 6" (15.2cm) blocks, you will need to piece 132 blocks. To make the quilt 6" bigger on all sides, you'll either need to make an additional 50 blocks or simply add a 6" border!Use a folded border to add a pop of colour to your quilt. Sometimes that's all that's needed to create harmony in a design.

Adding a plain or simple border

1 In an ideal world you will be able to use the size of border given in the pattern. This relies on accurate sewing throughout – if you're adding pieced borders you really need them to fit and there's no really satisfying way to fudge it. Measure through the centre of your quilt from top to bottom. Does it correspond with the pattern? If not, make a note of the measurement. Repeat the measuring process at ⅓ and ⅔ across the quilt.

2 Add the measurements together and divide by three (in other words, take several measurements and find the average).

3 Cut your border to this length.

4 Find the centre of the border and place a pin. Find the ¼ positions too and, again, place pins.

5 Find the ¼, ½ and ¾ positions on the side of your quilt and match up the pinned border.

6 Match the ends and pin too.

7 Pin well in between, easing any slight fullness throughout the seam.

8 Sew the border in place.

9 Press the border back then add the opposite border in the same way.

10 Repeat the measuring process through the width of the quilt and border to find the required length for the remaining two sides.

11 Don't be tempted to sew long strips of fabric to the sides of your quilt and trim the ends off. I know it's faster, but your quilt will probably end up wonky and rippled around the edges – not a good look and no fun to quilt!

12 You can also add borders with cornerstones or corner blocks. Each border is cut to the length or width of the quilt top and and then four cornerstones or corner blocks the same size as the border are added.

Adding a pieced border to a quilt

A lot of quilters shy away from these; they have a reputation for being harder to put on a quilt than a plain border. I think it's the opposite, but I understand why some quilters feel this way. If your method of adding a simple border is to sew long strips on and then trim the ends off to make it fit, adding a pieced border which *has* to fit – no trimming possible – will be much harder. But that's not the way to add borders as I've explained, and adding a pieced border that is already delineated into regular 'chunks' actually gives us easy opportunities to match up and spread out the border strips along the edge of the quilt top. Pieced borders add so much extra panache to a quilt and I think they are worth every minute of their construction!

Adding a mitred border

Mitred borders are like very special picture frames and are particularly effective if you are using a large-scale patterned fabric or a stripe. Rather than being cut off by a straight border, the stripe appears to bend around the corner.

1 Cut border strips that are the width required x length of the quilt and add twice the width of the border strip to the length, plus an extra couple of inches for insurance. For example, if the quilt side was 80" (203.2) and the border width was 8" (20.3cm) I'd cut a border strip 8" (20.3cm) x 80" (203.2) and add 16" (40cm) + 2" (5.1cm) to the length, so 98" (248.9cm) long.

2 Sew all the border strips in place, starting and ending each one ¼" (6mm) in from the raw edge of the quilt top.

3 Starting at one corner, fold the quilt top on the diagonal and line up the two border strips on top of each other, including the overhanging border.

4 Place a ruler on top of the overhang and line it up with the fold of the quilt top.

5 Mark a pencil line on the overhanging border strips, pin and then sew on this line from the very corner of the quilt to the outside edge.

6 Open the seam and check for fit. If you're happy, trim the excess border fabric leaving a ¼" (6mm) seam allowance or unpick and have another go. Repeat on the remaining three sides.

Adding a folded or 'flange' border

A flange border is a fine folded strip, inserted into a seam of a quilt.

1   Measure your quilt for the first folded border and cut pieces to size. For example, to add a flange in between a 4" (10.2cm) border and your quilt centre, you will need to cut regular border strips that measure 4 1/2" (11.4cm) x the length of your quilt top.

2   For your flange, cut 1" (2.5cm) strips of your flange fabric to the same length as your quilt, then fold this narrow strip in half, wrong sides together, and press.

3   Pin and baste (tack) this folded strip (the flange) to the edge of your quilt centre with the raw edges aligned and the fold pointing inwards towards the quilt centre.

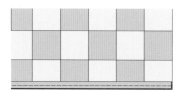

4   Repeat until the flange is attached to all four sides of your quilt. At the corners, simply overlap the folded strips.

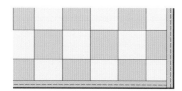

5   Pin your first border strip (in this case the 4½"/11.4cm strip) to the quilt side, overlapping the folded flange.

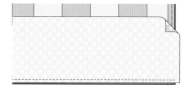

6   Sew the border on with a ¼" (6mm) seam.

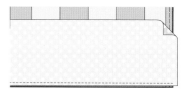

7   Press the border back to reveal a 4" (10.2cm) finished border with a narrow ¼" (6mm) folded flange captured in the seam.

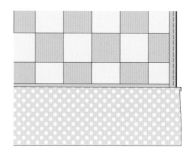

8   Repeat on the remaining three sides.

A flange can be other widths; just choose the finished width of the flange and double it, then add ½" (13mm) seam allowance to find the width of the strip you need to cut. For a ¾" (19mm) finished flange you would double ¾" (19mm), making 1½" (3.8cm) and add ½" (13mm) for before seam allowance. Cut strips at 2" (5cm) wide by however long your quilt side is.

Layering and basting your quilt

Once your quilt top is completed you're almost ready to layer and quilt – almost. Before you layer your quilt top there are a few jobs to be done.

1   Clip any threads that are hanging loose on the back or front of your quilt top.

2   Make sure that seams are well pressed and are lying flat. If any seams are twisted, unpick the twisted part, flatten and re-sew.

3   Sew around the outer edge of your quilt top about ⅛" (3mm) in from the raw edge to stabilise it.

4   Give your quilt top a final press.

Cut a piece of backing fabric for your quilt. It needs to be at least 2–3" (5–7.6cm) bigger on all sides than the quilt top. Piece the backing if necessary to get the required size. Make sure these seams are pressed open to reduce bulk and avoid a ridge.

Cut a piece of quilt batting to the same size as the backing fabric. It's a really good idea to open out your batting 24–48 hours before layering to allow the wrinkles to relax. Just lay it out over a spare bed for a day or so.

1   Lay your backing fabric down, wrong side up. Smooth out and tape at the edges with masking tape.

2   Lay your batting on top and smooth from the centre out to make sure it is flat and wrinkle free.

3   Lay your quilt top on top, right side facing up, centring the top with the batting and backing and placing it 2" (5cm) down from the top.

4   Use curved safety pins to hold the layers together. I try to make sure there is no more than a fist's width between the pins.

Alternatively use quilt basting spray to temporarily hold the layers of your 'quilt sandwich' together while you quilt. Follow the manufacturer's instructions.

Quilting the quilt

There's a saying among quilters that 'it's not a quilt until it's quilted', and this is certainly true in my book! A quilt consists of three layers: the top, the backing and a layer of batting in between. Machine or hand stitches through all three layers hold them together, and this is called the 'quilting'. Your chosen batting will recommend how far apart your lines of stitches need to be in order to hold the quilt together properly; as a guide, quilting should be evenly spread across the whole quilt surface to be aesthetically pleasing and functional. Quilting can be done by hand or machine and nowadays it can also be done by credit card. I shall explain!

Quilting by hand

Using a short betweens or quilting needle and a 16" (40cm) length of strong thread, sew a running stitch through the layers of the quilt. Start and finish with a small knot, which can be pulled into the middle of the quilt to hide it. Aim to keep your stitches even on the front and back. 'Big stitch' hand quilting is another popular choice and involves using cotton perle thread and a larger than usual running stitch to add decorative hand quilting to certain parts of your quilt.

Quilting by machine

Use a walking foot for straight lines and a darning foot for free motion swirls, shapes and stipples. Machine quilting can be as simple as sewing slightly to one side of all the main blocks and pieces in a quilt (quilting 'in the ditch') or can form an integral part of the overall design. The choices is yours. It's worth considering this as a separate skill to patchworking; there are a number of great books that specifically focus on this important technique.

Quilting by credit card

'Longarm quilting' is a very useful service offered by a number of professionals and is well worth considering if you do not enjoy or are daunted by the task of quilting on your domestic sewing machine. You send the top to a 'longarmer', who then professionally quilts your top for a fee and sends it back to you for binding. Make sure you discuss what you would like before sending your precious top away and follow the longarm quilter's directions for preparation to the letter!

Double-fold binding your quilt

I like to bind my quilts with double-fold binding cut at 2½" (6.4cm) on the straight of grain (see page 24). This gives a sturdy binding and is the most commonly used method of binding a quilt. Occasionally you may need to cut your strips on the bias or at 45 degrees to the straight of grain – this makes the binding strips much stretchier and is perfect if the quilt you are binding has curved edges.

1   Measure the four sides of your quilt together and add 10" (25.4cm) extra for corners and overlap. Cut strips of fabric from the widthwise or lengthwise grain of your fabric and piece together to reach this length. Use straight or diagonal seams and press the seams open to reduce bulk.

2   Fold the binding strip in half to create a strip that is 1¼" (3.2cm) wide, with the right sides of the fabric on the outside. Also fold the raw edges 1" (2.5cm) in on the leading end and press to neaten it.

3   Starting on the right side of the quilt and approximately 6" (15.2cm) down from a corner, pin the neatened end of the binding to the raw edge of the quilt.

4   Using a ¼" (6mm) seam allowance and beginning approximately 3" (7.6cm) down from the neatened edge, sew the binding to the first side of the quilt. Finish exactly ¼" (6mm) from the corner and backstitch to secure your thread.

5   Take the quilt out from your machine and clip your threads.

6   With the newly bound edge of your quilt at the top and the next edge to be bound on the right-hand side, take your binding strip up until it is in line with the next edge to be bound.

7   Fold the binding back down on itself and align the raw edges of the binding with the raw edge of the quilt. Pin at the corner.

8   Start sewing ¼" (6mm) in from the edge of the quilt and sew with a ¼" (6mm) seam until you get to a ¼" (6mm) of the next corner. Backstitch, remove your quilt from the machine and clip threads. Repeat for each side of the quilt.

9   When you get back to the first edge, make the last corner and sew approximately 2" (5cm) down. Backstitch and clip threads.

10 Trim the end of your binding strip, allowing about 1" (2.5cm) to tuck inside the neatened leading edge. Pin in place and sew the last few inches of your binding in place.

11 Once the binding has been machine sewn to the front of your quilt you can turn the folded edge to the back of your quilt and slip stitch in place by hand. It's a fairly slow process to do well but you will be left with an immaculate binding, which will finish your quilt to perfection.

Sometimes, especially for 'utility' projects, I'll machine the binding on both sides. To do this sew the binding to the right side as before, flip the binding to the wrong side and then, sewing from the right side again, sew 'in the ditch' between the binding and the quilt. Make sure that as you stitch you are catching the binding down at the back.

Adding a hanging sleeve

If you want to display your quilt on a wall or at a quilt show you will need to add a hanging sleeve to the back of your quilt. This is most easily done before you bind the quilt.

1   For most large quilts cut a strip of fabric 8½" (21.6cm) wide x the width of your quilt. For example, 8½" (21.6cm) x 80" (203.2cm). If you're working with a much smaller quilt you might want to cut a narrower hanging sleeve but if you intend on sending it to an exhibition or quilt show check with the organisers, who often have very exacting requirements to fit their hanging systems.

2   Fold the raw ends of the strip in ½" (13mm) and press, repeat to neaten the ends. Stitch in place. Fold the sleeve in half, wrong sides together, and press. The sleeve will now be 2" (5cm) shorter than the quilt and 4¼" (10.8cm) wide.

3   Align the raw edges of the sleeve with the top raw edge of your quilt, centring the sleeve, and baste (tack) in place.

4   Attach the binding to your quilt, simultaneously attaching the binding and the top of the sleeve in one step.

5   Hand sew the binding to the back of the quilt.

6   Hand sew the bottom edge of the hanging sleeve to the back of your quilt. Use small stitches and make sure they do not show on the front of your quilt.

7   Pass a rod or wooden batten through the sleeve to allow hanging.

Adding a label

It's a very good idea to add a label to the back of quilts and wall hangings, whether they are intended as gifts or not. The label can be a simple square or rectangle of plain fabric, hemmed and hand stitched to the back of the quilt. Use a fabric safe pen to write relevant information on the label...the makers name and the date it was started and finished...the name of the quilt and perhaps the recipient's details. In years to come, future generations will want to know the whos, whats and whys so let's make their job a little easier and remember to add the label!

A Sky Full of Stars

86" x 86"

Designed, pieced and quilted by Stuart Hillard
and completed October 2022
North Yorkshire, UK

"A sky full of stars" was inspired by my love
of the night sky, particularly on a cold and
clear autumn night when I can light a fire
wrap up warm and just sit and gaze into the sky
It's taken from my book "A year of Quilts from the country"
Published by Pavilion in 2024

Cutting fabric on the bias

Cutting on the bias – or across the woven grain – is done to utilise a fabric's natural 'stretchiness'. Find the 45 degree line on your rotary cutting ruler and place it so that it lines up with the selvedge or straight of grain on your fabric. This places the edge of the ruler at a 45 degree angle. Cut along the edge of your ruler and then cut strips from this cut edge. Usually you will cut strips at 2½" (6.4cm) for binding. Just be very careful how you handle the strips, because they will be very stretchy.

Covering seams with bias binding

This is particularly lovely on garments such as my Japanese Haori Jacket (see page 75) when the lining is quilted to the outer fabric and the inside seams need to be made neat and beautiful. You can buy ready-made bias binding or make your own using a bias tape maker. Open the binding out and fold one end in by ½" (13mm) to neaten it. Position the bias tape on the right side of the seam, raw edges aligned, and sew in the first fold of the tape to attach it to the garment or quilt. Turn the bias binding to the wrong/lining side of the garment and pin in place. Sew in place by hand with small slip stitches or sew from the right side, sewing just inside the edge of the bias tape to attach it at the back.

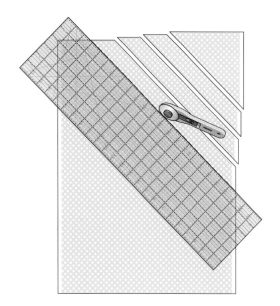

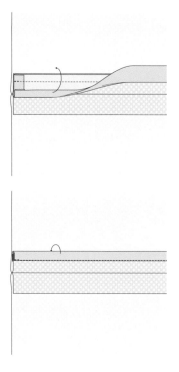

Joining fabrics with a diagonal seam

Generally I do this on binding strips and sometimes when I'm joining border strips the diagonal seam helps to distribute the seam allowance and prevents bulk in one area. It can also be harder to spot a diagonal seam, especially if you've matched patterns up carefully! Lay one strip down, right side facing up. Place the other strip on top, right sides together, at a right angle. I like to think of it as a backwards 'L'. Draw a diagonal line from corner to corner and pin. Sew on the line and then open the fabrics out. Press the seam allowances open and then trim them back to ¼" (6mm).

Making a pieced or split backing

Do this when you are making something padded like The Crazy Scrap Hanging Heart or Embroidered Tree Decoration (see pages 117 and 199). Conventional wisdom says to leave a gap at the side, which you use to stuff the shape, and then close by hand with a ladder stitch, but I never think this looks great. I sew two pieces of fabric together for the backing; cut a rectangle of fabric that's about 1" (2.5cm) bigger on all sides and then split it down the middle. Rejoin the two pieces but leave a 3" (7.6cm) gap in the very centre of the seam. Use this gap to stuff the shape and then hand sew closed. Your join is on the back and away from prying eyes!

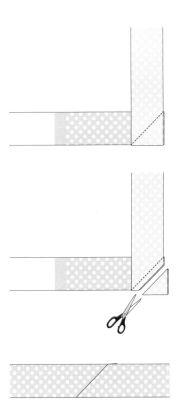

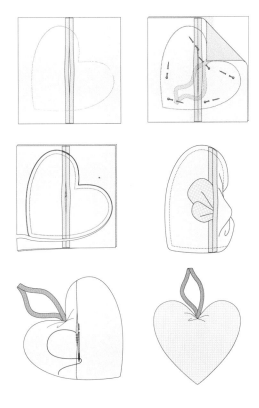

Sewing buttons

Use double thread to sew buttons and tie a knot in the end. Sew a couple of backstitches in place and then pass the needle up through one of the holes in the button and back down another. If the button has four holes, you can sew an X; make sure you sew each set of holes at least three times. I like to use embroidery floss to sew buttons; it's nice and strong and I sometimes leave the tail on top of my work, sew the button and then tie the ends off in a decorative knot on the top of the button. I also love stacking buttons and sewing two or three buttons of ascending size in a little tower. It's not functional, but it looks gorgeous!

Hand Embroidery

Backstitch

Use two strands of embroidery floss and a crewel or embroidery needle. Make a knot in the end of your floss. Bring the needle and thread to the surface of your work, go back down into the fabric taking one small straight stitch, come back up a thread's width in front of the first and then go back on yourself down the 'exit hole', making another stitch and filling in the gap. Come back up one stitch length ahead of this stitch and repeat.

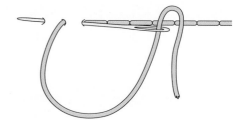

French knots

Bring the needle to the surface of your work, pull the thread taut and wrap it three times around the tip of the needle. Then insert the needle back down through the fabric a tiny distance from the exit hole, leaving the wrapped thread as a knot on the surface.

Ladder stitch

This is a hand stitch that invisibly closes a gap or joins two fabrics together. Use a single thread and tie a knot (which you can bury in the fabric). Bring the thread up at one side of the gap, just in the fold of the fabric. Pierce on the other side of the fold and pass the needle up, inside the fold, by about ¼" (6mm). Bring the needle out onto the surface of the fabric again, just inside the fold, pierce the fold of the fabric on the opposite side of the gap and again travel ¼" (6mm) inside the fold before bringing the needle back out onto the surface of the fabric. You're creating little horizontal 'rungs' of a ladder across the gap. Pull them up tight as you go and do a couple of backstitches to finish.

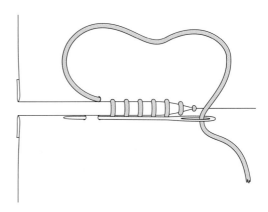

Making an envelope backing

This is a very easy way to make a cushion backing and requires no zip and no special skills! Cut two backing pieces for your cushion. I like to cut mine to the width of the cushion front x two-thirds the length, which gives a good overlap. On the inside edge, essentially where the panels will overlap, fold then press a double ½" (13mm) hem. Top stitch this hem and press neatly. Arrange the panels, right sides facing down, against the right side of the cushion front with neatened edges overlapping in the centre and the raw edges aligned around the outside edge. Pin the outside edge and then sew with a ¼" (6mm) seam allowance. Turn through to the right side and check your seams. If everything looks good, turn it back through to the wrong side and neaten the raw edges of the cushion cover with an overlocker or a wide zigzag stitch.

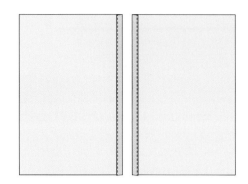

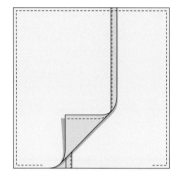

Making covered piping cord

I use ⅜" (1cm) diameter cotton cord, ideal for cushions. Tie a fat knot on one end to stop the cord pulling through. Cut 1" (2.5cm) wide strips of fabric to cover the cord and join with diagonal seams. Wrap the fabric around the cord and bring the flat raw edges together on the right-hand side. Using the zipper foot on your machine, sew close to the cord.

Position and pin cord in place with the raw edges aligned and the piping cord facing inwards. Snip into the fabric that covers the cord at the corners to allow you to bend it then baste and finally sew the cord in place using the zip foot on your machine. I criss-cross the start/finish ends to create a neat finish without having to join them. Add your envelope back to the cushion then sew as close to the piping cord as possible.

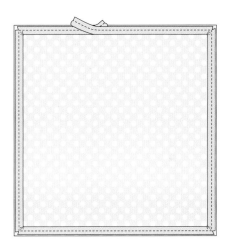

General advice for starting your quilt

One of the best tips I could give any quilter is to start with just one block rather than launching into cutting and piecing an entire quilt. Making one block will help you to test your cutting and piecing accuracy, may influence the method you use with the rest of the quilt and feels like a quick finish too, which I find very motivating!

Before using fabrics give them a light spritz with spray starch and then press well to firm the fabric up. This helps enormously when you're piecing triangles.

I can't over-emphasise how important it is to measure your block. Ensure you do this throughout the process of making any quilt. I want my quilts and your quilts to go together like a dream not a nightmare – and that means accuracy! If your blocks aren't coming out the correct size check out my tips on page 32.

How to use this book

The projects in this book span a whole year of country quilting. There are projects for every season and colourways and designs to suit my four favourite country styles. The projects are rated by level of difficulty – I always have mixed feelings about doing this as I don't want anyone to feel that a project is labelled 'not for you', so use these ratings as a guide only. I've also included a list of 'skills used' at the start of every project so if there's anything there which is brand new to you, have a look on pages 21–53 and do a little practice before embarking on a more complex project.

Mix and match the projects, seasons and styles. My versions are simply that, one interpretation of the pattern (and sometimes two or three because I couldn't help myself!). Feel free to cross-pollinate one project with a different style or season. Bed quilts can be made larger or smaller with the addition or subtraction of blocks or borders, a table runner or cushion could be the start of a much bigger project and you can even mix and match the blocks or substitute one for another. Above all, I look forward to seeing your versions of these projects, large or small, whatever your personal style is!

My heart is most definitely in the country and the projects in this book have a very definite rural flavour, but many of them would look incredible reinterpreted in a modern, brighter or more pared-down palette, so if you are in need of a project for a city dweller (perhaps yourself), look no further. Finally, if I have learned nothing else in over thirty years of quilting it is this:

Fabric maketh the project!

The Fisherman's Nook

in *Spring*

Springtime on the coast is all about freshness and newness. There are clear, pale blue skies and gentle rain, longer days for walking the cliff paths, daffodils along every lane and a sense that the countryside is coming back to life. Cobbled lanes weave between the houses and at every turn you catch a glimpse of the sea, sparkling in the early spring light. An old anchor propped against a wall and a ship's lantern hanging from the ceiling tell you that you've arrived at the Fisherman's Nook.

At this ancient cottage nestled in winding lanes, spring's lightness and brightness, the blue of the sky and the sea are all reflected in the projects in this chapter. In The Fisherman's Catch Embroidered Quilt, a net of patchwork chains capture shells and starfish, a length of twisted rope and an old ship in a bottle is rendered in bluework embroidery (worked in blue floss on a natural background). A beady-eyed blue crab watches from my Catch of the Day Cushion, and makes the perfect bedfellow for the She Sells Seashells Cushion, adorned with appliqué starfish and mother-of-pearl buttons. The ship's compass on my Where the Wind Blows You Quilt guides the way to a bounty of pieced star blocks while geese fly overhead, returning for spring. The fresh Atlantic winds bring the Flotsam and Jetsam Cushion to the beach and a chill to the air, but my warm quilted Japanese Haori Jacket and Patchwork and Quilted Slippers are sure to keep you warm until summer.

Coastal *Country* Style

Coastal country decor takes its inspiration from the land and the sea, the colours of the sky and the natural elements. Warm sandy tones, whitewashed walls, and natural wood mixed with nautical navy and white stripes, shells, sea glass and driftwood create the perfect contemporary look. The coastal style is all about mixing the colours of the beach with finds – an old brass ship's light or a wooden chest used as a table, shells in a jar or glass floats hung in a window.

I've used lots of different shades of blue in the projects included in this chapter, from a navy so dark it's almost black right through to the softest whisper of sky blue, and of course, every blue in between! For contrast I've chosen white, a very clean and bright cream and a warmer tan, reminiscent of sand and seashells.

I've also chosen fabric styles that reflect the theme: checks, plaids, ikat weaves and bali batiks sit next to British vintage-style florals and small geometrics. There's a healthy dose of traditional Japanese-style cloths too, such as woven stripes, shibori dyed fabrics and hand-stitched or printed sashiko. So many of these use indigo and rich blues as their palette and have a beautiful contemporary country style which is perfect for the projects in this chapter. And stripes – it wouldn't be coastal without the seaside's characterisitics stripes, be they simple, deckchair inspired or nautical. Stripes are essential!

Where the Wind Blows You Quilt

ADVANCED

I love to travel and my work and wanderlust have taken me all over the world. Everywhere I go I meet other quilters and our shared love of patchwork always makes me feel at home. This is a showstopper of a quilt featuring one big beautiful mariner's compass block in the centre and four smaller star blocks at the corners. It looks beautiful made in navy, aqua and sky blue mixed with plenty of soft cream and tan but it would look equally wonderful in scrappy rich jewel tones on a navy or black background, so don't be afraid to embrace the colours of the world! No matter where the wind blows you, if you have a quilt with you, you're home!

This is advanced level sewing and you'll need to be familiar with both paper foundation piecing (see page 33) and sewing with templates. Take your time, enjoy the process and make yourself an heirloom.

PROJECT SIZE

Finished quilt 68 x 68" (172.7 x 172.7cm)

Centre block size 30½ x 30½" (77.5 x 77.5cm)

Number of centre blocks 1

Setting block size 12 x 12" (30.5 x 30.5cm)

Number of setting blocks 4

- See pullout sheet for templates

YOU WILL NEED

- 3 metres light cream background fabric; you can use all the same fabric if you wish or use the equivalent in fat quarters if you prefer
- 1 metre warm tan print
- 2 fat quarters of dark blue prints for the medium and large compass points
- 2 fat quarters of light or medium blue prints for the medium and large compass points. You can use the leftovers in your blocks, small compass points and flying geese borders
- Approximately 8 fat quarters of medium dark and very dark blue prints for the small compass points and block/cornerstone piecing

- Approximately 8 fat quarters of light blue and light aqua prints for the block piecing and the flying geese border
- ½ metre aqua/light blue/navy wide stripe for block border
- ½ metre very dark navy print for the inner border
- ¾ metre very dark navy print for the binding
- 74 x 74" (188 x 188cm) quilt batting
- 74 x 74" (188 x 188cm) backing fabric
- Thread for piecing and quilting
- Template material
- Spray starch

SKILLS USED

- Using templates
- Paper foundation piecing
- Simple patchwork
- Adding borders and cornerstones
- Setting blocks 'on point'
- Adding pieced borders
- Layering and quilting
- Binding a quilt

Continue overleaf...

Let's make the quilt!

Remember to use a shorter than usual stitch when sewing foundations, or a regular patch or border to a foundation, to make the paper easy to remove. Make copies of all the templates on template plastic or freezer paper. Always place templates on the right side of your fabric for cutting out.

Make the centre compass block

It's a really good idea to spray starch and press the fabrics used for the large and medium compass points before cutting out. It will make the fabrics so much easier to work with; they will behave better and press more crisply.

1   Make eight copies of the Small Compass Points foundation and using the foundation paper piecing method, sew these units. Use assorted dark blue prints for the slip points and a light cream background print for the larger points (background). Trim each foundation to the dotted seam allowance line.

2   Using cream background fabric cut eight of template G. Transfer the two red dots with an erasable pen.

3   Sew the G template shapes to the bottom of each of the foundation paper pieced units, aligning the marked dots on G with the bottom points of the compass section. Press seams towards the G shape.

4   Use template C to cut four dark blue medium points, use template D to cut four light blue medium points, use template E to cut four cream triangles and template F to cut a further four cream triangles.

5   Sew a cream E triangle to the bottom of a C medium compass point and press the seam towards the dark fabric. Repeat to make four. Sew a cream F triangle to the bottom of a D medium compass point and press the seam towards the cream fabric. Repeat to make four.

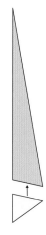

6   Cut four A template large compass points in dark blue and four B template large compass points in light blue.

7   Sew the C/E sections made in step 5 to the right-hand side of four of the small compass points foundations and then a B template to the left side of each foundation unit. Press.

8 Sew one F/D section to the left-hand side of each of the remaining four small compass points foundations and an A template to the right side of each foundation unit. Press seams open.

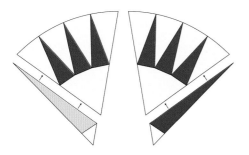

9 Join the sections together into quarters, along the line which joins the A and B templates (or large compass points) together. Press seams open.

12 Join the four quarter blocks together and press the seams open. Quilt block measures 31" x 31" (78.7 x 78.7cm).

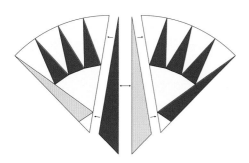

10 From cream background fabric cut four background quarter blocks, transferring the red dots from the template to the fabric with an erasable pen.

11 Aligning the compass points with the red dots on the background fabric, sew a compass section to a background quarter block – pin this seam really well and sew slowly! Press the seam allowance towards the background quarter block. Repeat to make four.

13 From striped border print cut four strips each 2½" x 31" (6.4 x 78.7cm) and from dark blue print cut four cornerstones each 2½" x 2½" (6.4 x 6.4cm).

14 Sew border strips to two opposite sides of the centre block and press the seam allowance towards the striped border. Sew a cornerstone to either end of the remaining border strips and press the seam allowance towards the striped border. Sew the last two border strips with cornerstones

to the last two sides of the quilt centre and press the seam allowances towards the striped border. Quilt measures 35" x 35" (89 x 89cm) at this point.

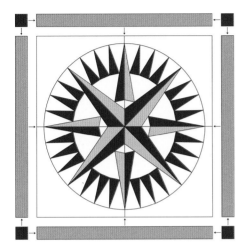

Make the setting blocks

There are four of these blocks to make and each one will be 12 x 12" (30.5 x 30.5cm).

1   Make 16 copies of the Flying Geese Plus foundation. Use light aqua blue for the large triangles, deep navy for the square and light cream print for the background/small triangles. Piece 16 Flying Geese Plus units and trim to the dotted seam allowance line.

2   Make four copies of the Complex Square in a Square foundation. Use light cream print for the centre square and outer large triangles and your deepest navy print for the inner triangles.

3   From light cream background print, cut 16 squares each 3½ x 3½" (8.9 x 8.9cm).

4   Arrange four Flying Geese Plus units around the centre Complex Square in a Square unit and four plain cream print squares at the corners. Sew the units together and press the seams in alternate rows in opposite directions. Sew the rows together and press. Your block should measure 12½ x 12½" (31.7 x 31.7cm) at this stage. Repeat to make four.

5   Create the setting triangles by cutting two large 18¼ x 18¼" (46.3 x 46.3cm) squares from light cream fabric and cutting on both diagonals to yield a total of eight triangles. Sash two opposite sides of the blocks with these triangles and then cut two 9½" (24.1cm) squares of light cream print and cut each once on the diagonal to yield a total of four corner triangles. Sew one corner triangle to the other side of the block and trim the dog ears. Make four setting triangles in total. Mark the centre of each setting triangle with a pin.

6   Find the centre of each side of the quilt centre and mark with a pin. Line up the centre mark of the setting triangles and then sew two of the setting triangles to opposite sides of the quilt centre and press the seams towards the triangles. Sew the remaining two setting triangles to the last two sides of the quilt centre and press the seams towards the setting triangles. Quilt centre measures 50½ x 50½" (128.2 x 128.2cm) at this stage.

Add two plain borders to the quilt

1 Use the first border dark blue print to cut six strips each 1½" (3.8cm) x width of fabric and join end to end with diagonal seams. From this length cut two pieces 1½ x 50½" (3.8 x 128.2cm) and two strips 1½ x 52½" (3.8 x 133.4cm).

2 Sew the shorter borders to two opposite sides of the quilt and press the seams towards the border, then sew the longer border strips to the remaining two sides of the quilt and press as before. Quilt now measures 52½ x 52½" (133.4 x 133.4cm).

3 Add the second plain border, this time in light cream background fabric. Cut six strips each 2½" (6.4cm) x width of fabric and join end to end with diagonal seams; from this strip cut two strips 2½ x 52½" (6.4 x 133.4cm) and two strips each 2½ x 56½" (6.4 x 143.5cm). Sew the shorter strips to the shorter sides of the quilt and press and then add the longer border strips to the two remaining sides and press. Quilt centre now measures 56½ x 56½" (143.5 x 143.5cm).

Make the outer flying geese borders

1 Make eight copies of Flying Geese x 5 foundation and 16 copies of Flying Geese x 4 foundation. Use assorted light aqua and blue prints for the large 'geese' and warm tan print for the small triangle 'sky'. Use the foundation piecing technique to piece all 24 foundations – trim each foundation to the dotted seam allowance lines and then sew together two of the Flying Geese x 4 and one of the Flying Geese x 5 units to make a line of thirteen geese. Make eight of these geese border units.

2 Make eight copies of the Simple Square in a Square foundation. Use dark navy blue for the centre patch and warm tan print for the small triangles. Piece the eight units and trim to the dotted seam allowance lines.

3 Sew one geese border unit either side of a Simple Square in a Square unit. Repeat to make four. Sew a Simple Square in a Square unit to either end of two of the geese borders.

4 Sew the shorter flying geese borders to two opposite sides of the quilt centre and press seams to the plain inner border. Sew the remaining longer flying geese borders to the last two sides of the quilt and press the seams towards the plain inner border. Quilt measures 64½ x 64½" (163.8 x 163.8cm) at this stage.

Sew the final plain border to the quilt

1   From light cream print cut two strips each
    2½ x 64½" (6.4 x 163.8cm) and sew these
    to two opposite sides of the quilt. Press the
    seam allowances towards the plain border.
    Cut two strips each 2½" x 68½" (6.4 x 174cm)
    for the last two sides of the quilt – sew to
    the quilt and press. Quilt top now measures
    68½" x 68½" (174 x 174cm).

2   Remove all foundation papers and press
    your quilt top.

3   Layer your quilt top with batting and
    backing fabric and quilt as desired. I
    quilted a 'Japanese wave' pattern across
    the surface of the quilt. Straight line echo
    quilting around your perfect piecing would
    also look wonderful and show off your
    workmanship!

4   Trim your batting and backing fabrics
    even with the quilt top. From your binding
    fabric cut eight strips each 2½" (6.4cm) x
    width of fabric (42"/106.7cm) and join them
    with diagonal seams. Use this strip to bind
    your quilt.

5   Add a label to the back of the quilt.

6   Stand back and admire your work and as
    you look at those compass points remember
    – East, West, Quilting's Best!

The Fisherman's Catch
Embroidered Quilt

INTERMEDIATE

The Fisherman's Catch quilt was inspired by holidays spent in our friends' cottage in the fishing village of Robin Hood's Bay. As soon as the tide went out we'd go rock pooling, searching for shells, sea glass and the occasional crab left behind by the waves. Twisted ropes, an old ship's wheel and a ship in a bottle placed high on a shelf bring the sounds, the smells and the tranquillity of the coast straight to my mind and calmness to my soul.

This quilt is an absolute delight to make. Enjoy a relaxing time while hand sewing the embroidery blocks in the fresh spring light and then machine sewing the patchwork and blocks together in a weekend. The border is integrated into the design so once the blocks are sewn together you're ready to layer and quilt!

PROJECT SIZE

Finished quilt 50 x 50" (127 x 127cm)

Block size 10 x 10" (25.4 x 25.4cm)

Number of embroidered blocks 5

Number of pieced blocks 12

· See pullout sheet for templates

YOU WILL NEED

· A minimum of 5 fat quarters of assorted light creams for the embroidery backgrounds and patchwork piecing, plus approximately 3 fat quarters of scraps to make the patchwork

· 1 metre light fusible woven interfacing

· Assorted navy scraps for the piecing, equivalent to 1½ metres, 6 fat quarters or 12 fat eighths

· ¼ metre light aqua print for the pieced blocks

· 1 metre large-scale navy floral for the large plain blocks and the block piecing

· ½ metre blue and navy striped fabric for the binding

· 57 x 57" (144.8 x 144.8cm) quilt batting

· 57 x 57" (144.8 x 144.8cm) quilt backing fabric

· Thread to piece and quilt

· Assorted light and dark blue embroidery floss skeins (variegated floss would look lovely too)

· Crewel needle and 9" (22.9cm) embroidery hoop

· Template material

SKILLS USED

· Hand embroidery

· Simple patchwork

· Layering and quilting

· Adding a double-fold binding

Continue overleaf...

Let's make the quilt!

1   Start by cutting one 14 x 14" (35.6 x 35.6cm)
    square from each of the five fat quarters of
    light background fabrics. Save the remainder
    of the fat quarters for the patchwork piecing.
    Find the centre of each square and mark the
    five embroidery designs using a fine pencil
    or fabric-safe pen. Cut five 14 x 14" (35.6 x
    35.6cm) squares of light interfacing and fuse
    one to the back of each square.

2   Using the general instructions for
    embroidery (see page 50) work each of the
    designs in a neat backstitch and use French
    knots to pick out the small dots. Note that
    the small circles on designs such as the
    starfish are worked in a backstitch. Only use
    French knots for dots.

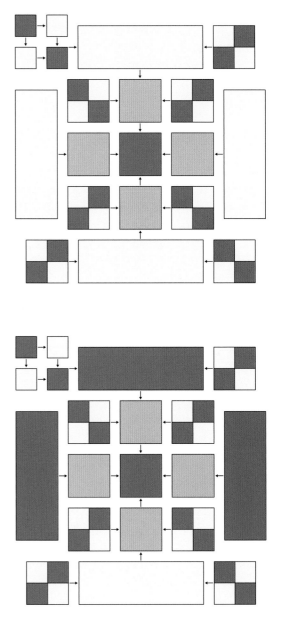

3 Press each embroidery carefully from the reverse then centre and trim each embroidery to a 10½ x 10½" (26.7 x 26.7cm) square. Set aside.

4 Make the patchwork blocks next. There are two colourways of the same block.

5 Start by making easy four-patch units. You need to make a total of 96 units, each measuring 2½ x 2½" (6.4 x 6.4cm). Cut lots of 1½ x 1½" (3.8 x 3.8cm) squares of blue and cream fabrics and sew them together – this is the best way to use small scraps, but if you have larger pieces of fabric then cut 1½" (3.8cm) strips that are as long as the piece of fabric. Pair a cream and a blue strip, right sides together, and sew with a ¼" (6mm) seam allowance. Press the seams towards the dark fabric, then cut again into 1½" (3.8cm) segments. Combine two different pairings to make each four-patch. You'll need eight four-patch units for each of the 12 blocks.

6 From the light aqua print cut a total of 48 2½ x 2½" (6.4 x 6.4cm) squares, four for each of the 12 blocks.

7 From the large-scale floral print cut eight 10½ x 10½" (26.7 x 26.7cm) squares for the outer blocks and 28 rectangles, each 2½ x 6½" (6.4 x 16.5cm), for the block piecing. From the assorted cream fabrics cut 20 rectangles, each 2½ x 6½" (6.4 x 16.5cm), for the block piecing.

8 Use your four-patch units, light aqua squares and a combination of navy floral and assorted cream rectangles to piece eight block As and four block Bs.

9 Arrange your embroidered blocks, your block As and Bs and your plain floral blocks as shown in five rows of five. Sew the blocks together and press the seams in opposite directions.

10 Layer your quilt top with backing and batting and quilt as desired. I quilted a large meandering line all over the surface to create great texture without distracting from the embroidery.

11 Trim your quilt backing and batting even with the quilt top.

12 Cut a total of six strips of binding fabric each 2½" (6.4cm) x width of fabric and join end to end using a diagonal seam. Press the seams open, then fold and press the strips in half. Use to bind the quilt using the directions for double-fold binding (see page 45).

13 Add a label to the quilt.

For another look substitute a large-scale floral print or a toile de Jouy for the embroideries and increase the size to eight blocks x eight blocks (64 in total) to create a romantic 80 x 80" (203.2 x 203.2cm) quilt for your bed.

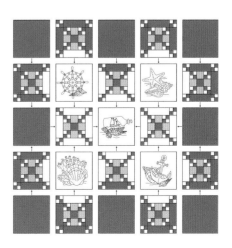

Catch of the Day Cushion

INTERMEDIATE

A gorgeous accent cushion that complements The Fisherman's Catch Embroidered Quilt (see page 68) to perfection but works really well as a standalone piece. Use the pattern as a base. Any of the embroideries from the Fisherman's Catch could be substituted, or you could replace the embroidery with a large-scale floral print and give the pillow a completely different look.

PROJECT SIZE

Finished quilt 18 x 18" (45.7 x 45.7cm)

· See pullout sheet for templates

YOU WILL NEED

· 14 x 14" (35.6 x 35.6cm) background fabric for the embroidery
· 14 x 14" (35.6 x 35.6cm) light fusible woven interfacing
· 1 skein variegated blue embroidery floss
· Crewel needle and 9" (22.9cm) embroidery hoop
· Assorted dark blue scraps for the pieced border
· 1 fat quarter of aqua and navy print for the outer border
· ½ metre coordinating fabric for the envelope back, or two contrasting fat quarters
· ¼ metre navy strip for the binding
· Threads for piecing and quilting
· 20 x 20" (50.8 x 50.8cm) quilt batting
· 20 x 20" (50.8 x 50.8cm) light cotton fabric to back the cushion front
· 18 x 18" (45.7 x 45.7cm) cushion pad (pillow form)
· Template material

SKILLS USED

· Hand embroidery
· Simple patchwork
· Layering and quilting
· Making an envelope back
· Joining strips with a diagonal seam
· Double-fold binding

Let's make the cushion!

1   Find the centre of the 14 x 14" (35.6 x 35.6cm) background square then trace the crab design onto the right side using a light pencil or fabric-safe marking pen. Iron the interfacing to the back of the background square.

2   Hoop the fabric and, using two strands of embroidery floss throughout, work the design using a neat backstitch. Follow the instructions for hand embroidery on page 50 if this is new to you.

3   Once the design is completed, carefully press your embroidery from the reverse and square up to 10½ x 10½" (26.7 x 26.7cm), making sure that the design is centred.

4   From the dark navy scraps cut eight rectangles each 2½ x 5½" (6.4 x 14cm) and four squares each 2½ x 2½" (6.4 x 6.4cm).

5   Sew two rectangles together. Repeat to make four border pieces. Sew one of these border pieces to opposite sides of the embroidered centre and press the seam allowances towards the border. Sew a 2½ x 2½" (6.4 x 6.4cm) square to either end of the remaining border units and press the seams towards the rectangles. Sew these border strips and cornerstones to the remaining two sides of the embroidered centre.

Continue overleaf...

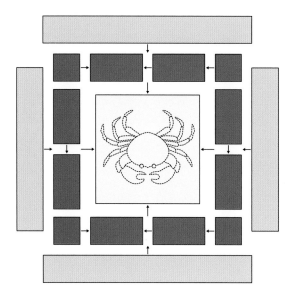

8 Make the envelope back next. From the backing fabric cut two rectangles each 14 x 18½" (35.6 x 47cm). Turn a double 2½" (6.4cm) hem along one 18½" (47cm) edge and press, then topstitch. Arrange the envelope backing onto the back of the cushion front with the pretty side of the backing fabrics facing up. This is different to the usual way of adding an envelope backing and that's because we are not turning through – we are going to bind the edge, just like a quilt.

9 Pin then baste the backing in place, less than ¼" (6mm) in from the raw edges.

10 Cut two strips of binding fabric each 2½" (6.4cm) x width of fabric (42"/106.7cm) and join them end to end using a diagonal seam. Fold the binding strip in half lengthwise and press. also neaten one end by turning a ½" (13mm) hem and pressing.

6 From your aqua and navy print cut two strips each 2½ x 14½" (6.4 x 37.8cm) and two pieces each 2½ x 18½" (6.4 x 47cm). Sew the outer border to the cushion front in the same manner as before.

7 Layer your cushion front with batting and a light plain cotton backing fabric. Quilt as desired. I stitched a simple meandering line all over the surface of the cushion front. A simple all-over quilting pattern will add lots of lovely texture but still allows your embroidery to shine. Trim the backing and batting even with the cushion front.

11 Bind the edge of your cushion just as you would a quilt. Sew the binding to the front of the cushion first by machine and then either hand sew the binding to the backing or sew by machine.

12 Insert the 18" (45.7cm) pad, plump your cushion and enjoy a life on the ocean waves!

Japanese Haori Jacket

INTERMEDIATE

My patchwork and quilted jacket is inspired by Haori, or quilted Japanese jackets, which are just perfect for beating those chilly spring nights. They were traditionally worn over a kimono by both men and women, but my jacket is equally at home worn over jeans and a T-shirt or a jersey dress and woollen tights. The Haori is roomy and will fit most shapes and sizes, although it's easy enough to shorten or lengthen the lower hem and sleeves if you wish. It comes complete with a smart neck, sleeve and bottom band and deep patch pockets for important things like keeping hands warm and sweets. I pieced a full 3 metres of patchwork before quilting it using the longarm method, but you could make smaller pieces of patchwork that are big enough to quilt on your domestic sewing machine and then cut individual pattern pieces if that is easier for you.

PROJECT SIZE

One size fits most
· See pullout sheet for templates

YOU WILL NEED

· 20 fat quarters of assorted navy, indigo and deep blue prints, sashiko-style fabrics, shibori-style prints, plaids and florals for the outer Haori
· 1 fat quarter of fabric for the patch pockets
· 3 metres quilt-weight cotton for the jacket lining
· 1¼ metre coordinating deep navy striped fabric for the neck facings, pocket linings, bottom edge and cuffs
· 1 metre medium-weight fusible interfacing
· 44" (111.7cm) x 3 metres thin cotton quilt batting
· Dressmaker's tissue for the pattern pieces
· 4 metres 1" (2.5cm) ready-made bias binding
· Thread for piecing, quilting and topstitching
· Template material

SKILLS USED

· Simple patchwork
· Layering and quilting
· Using templates/pattern pieces
· Using ready-made made bias binding to bind seams

Let's make the Haori Jacket!

Use a ⅝" (1.6cm) seam allowance throughout for the jacket construction but a ¼" (6mm) seam allowance for the patchwork fabric.

1   From the 20 fat quarters cut a total of 60 rectangles each 5½ x 16½" (14 x 41.9cm). Arrange the rectangles into eight alternating rows of six rectangles and seven rectangles and then use the remaining four rectangles, cut in half, to fill in the gaps at the top and bottom of the rows of six. Join the rectangles into rows and then join the rows together to make a piece of patchwork approximately 40½ x 112" (102.9 x 284.5cm).

Continue overleaf...

2 Layer your patchwork with batting and backing, baste together and then quilt as desired. I used a Japanese-style Baptist fan quilting motif. Straight-line quilting ⅛" (3mm) from each of the long seamlines would also look great and is easy to quilt with a walking foot on your sewing machine.

3 Cut the pattern pieces from dressmaker's tissue and then lay them out on your quilted fabric. Cut out the back, left and right front and two sleeves and transfer the pocket placement markings and the sleeve and shoulder notches.

4 From your extra fat quarter, cut out two patch pockets.

5 From your coordinating fabric cut two pocket linings, two cuff pieces, two neck facing pieces and two bottom band pieces. Cut corresponding pieces from the interfacing and fuse them to the wrong side of all the fabric pieces. Join both the neck facing pieces at the centre back. Join both pieces for the lower hem edging, again at the centre back seam. Press the seams open.

6 Take one pocket piece and one pocket lining and place right sides together, matching the top edges. Sew with a ¾" (19mm) seam allowance. Press the seam towards the lining fabric. Now bring the lower edges of the pocket pieces together, right sides touching. This will offset the top hem, creating a faux binding along the pocket top. Press. Pin and sew the side and bottom seams of the pocket, leaving a 3" (7.6cm) gap in one of the side seams. Turn through to the right side and turn the raw edges of the opening in to neaten, then press. Make a second pocket in the same way. Position the pockets on the jacket fronts and baste in place, then topstitch very close to the sides and base of the pocket. I like to sew a small triangle at the top of each pocket to reinforce this high-wear area.

Continue overleaf...

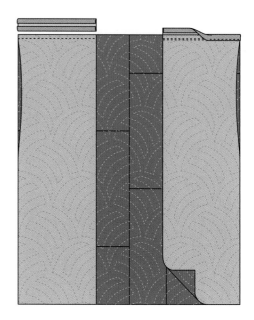

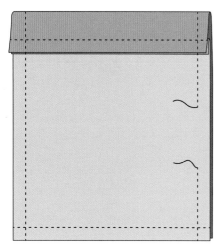

8 Lay the jacket back and fronts flat on a table. Position one sleeve, matching the centre fold of the sleeve with the shoulder seam. Pin in place, right sides together, and sew the sleeve in 'flat', starting and finishing your seam ⅝" (1.6cm) in from the raw edge of the sleeve. Repeat with the second sleeve, binding the seams as before.

7 With right sides together, place the left and right fronts on the jacket back, matching raw edges and shoulder notches. Pin, then sew the shoulder seams. Bind the shoulder seams with the ready-made bias tape by opening the binding out and first sewing to the right side of the seam following the fold in the bias tape, then flipping the tape to the other side of the seam, covering the raw edges, and machine sewing the binding in place.

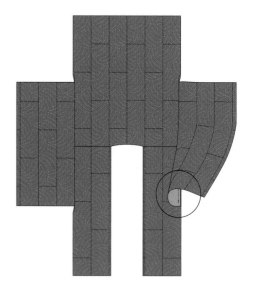

9 Sew the sleeve seams from cuff to underarm, finishing ⅝" (1.6cm) from the underarm as before. Repeat with the other sleeve and bind the seams.

wrong sides together, and press. Position the folded edge of the cuff over your original line of stitching and then either topstitch from the front 'in the ditch' to secure the cuff in place or hand stitch to the inside of the sleeve.

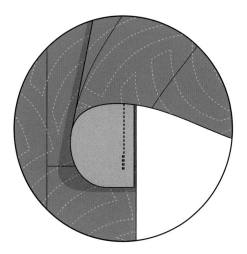

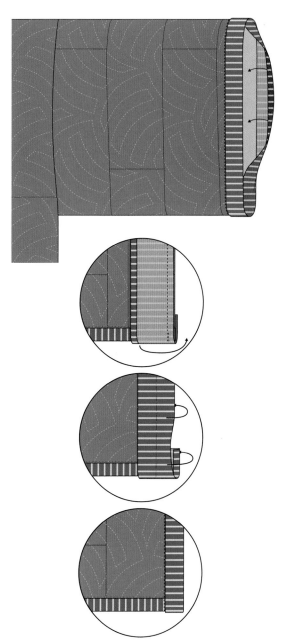

10 Sew the side seams, starting at the lower hem and finishing ⅝" (1.6cm) from the underarm seam. Bind the seams.

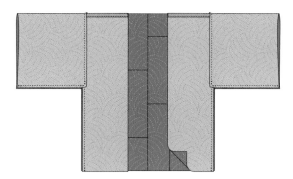

11 Take one of the cuff pieces and join into a circle using a ⅝" (1.6cm) seam allowance. Pin and sew the cuff to the raw edge of the sleeve using a ⅝" (1.6cm) seam allowance. Turn a ⅝" (1.6cm) hem along the raw edge of the cuff and then fold the cuff in half,

12 Sew the hem facing to the bottom of the jacket using a ⅝" (1.6cm) seam allowance. It's deliberately cut a little longer than needed so once it is stitched on, trim the front edges even with the centre fronts of the jacket. Turn ⅝" (1.6cm) in along the lower raw edge of the facing and press to neaten. Fold the hem facing in half and press.

13 Cover your original line of stitching with the neatened edge of the facing and pin in place. Topstitch from the front of the jacket next to the seam, making sure your stitches catch the folded edge of the facing on the lining side. Alternatively you can slip stitch the hem of the facing to the inside of the jacket by hand. Trim the edges.

14 Pin the neck facing to the front edges of the jacket, positioning the centre back seam of the facing with the centre back of the jacket. The facing is deliberately a little too long at the lower hems. To create a neat finish, fold the excess back around to the lining side and pin in place. Sew the facing to the jacket fronts using a ⅝" (1.6cm) seam allowance. Fold a ⅝" (1.6cm) seam allowance along the raw edge of the facing and press, then press the facing in half. Turn the neatened edge to the lining side and use the folded edge to just cover the original line of stitching. Hand stitch the facing in place or sew from the front 'in the ditch' to attach the facing to the lining side.

15 Give your Haori Jacket a light press and then pop it on.

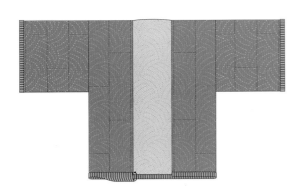

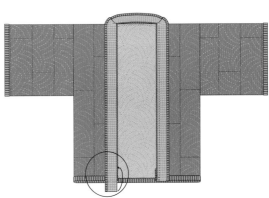

Flotsam and Jetsam Pillow

BEGINNER

Just like the flotsam and jetsam that is washed up on the seashore by the waves, my pillow incorporates a variety of discarded bits and bobs to make something really beautiful. I was inspired by Japanese boro patchwork where oddments, offcuts and even rags are sewn together in irregular rectangles with occasional appliquéd patches on top. Gather up odd squares and strips in coordinating colours or prints and sew them together in a haphazard way to create a bigger piece of new 'fabric'. The fabric is then quilted with batting and backing; traditionally this would be done with lines of hand stitching, very close together. Nowadays a similar effect can be created by machine in a fraction of the time. This is a technique rather than a very strict pattern and can be adapted to make quilt blocks, cushions of assorted sizes, quilted clothing and accessories such as bags.

PROJECT SIZE
Finished pillow 20 x 20" (50.8 x 50.8cm)

YOU WILL NEED
- Assorted scraps, strips, squares and offcuts of coordinating fabrics for the pillow front. I included some mock boro-style patchwork fabric along with my scraps to add extra variety
- ½ metre coordinating fabric for the pillow backing
- 25 x 25" (63.5 x 63.5cm) quilt batting
- 25 x 25" (63.5 x 63.5cm) plain cotton fabric or quilter's calico for the pillow backing
- 90 (228.6cm) cotton piping cord, ⅜" (1cm) diameter
- 1 fat quarter of coordinating fabric to cover the piping cord
- 20 x 20" (50.8 x 50.8cm) cushion pad (pillow form)
- Matching sewing thread

SKILLS USED
- Simple patchwork
- Quilting
- Joining strips with diagonal seams
- Covered piping cord edge
- Envelope back

Continue overleaf...

Let's make the pillow!

Use a ¼" (6mm) seam allowance throughout.

1 We are aiming to make an approximately 22 x 22" (55.9 x 55.9cm) square of patchwork fabric. I like to start by looking at my scraps and seeing what I've got. The larger pieces I might keep big, particularly if the fabric has a nice bold motif that I want to feature.

2 Trim the first large piece so that it is a square or rectangle. Sew other smaller squares, strips and rectangles together to make a piece of patchwork that is a little wider than your large square or rectangle. Trim the edges of the patchwork piece to fit the original square or rectangle and sew the fabrics together.

3 Add another patched piece of fabric to the unit until it measures approximately 22" (55.9cm) in length. The width doesn't really matter at this point.

4 Make a second patchwork strip using the same method. Trim the sides evenly. The length needs to be approximately 22" (55.9cm) as before.

5 Lay the two patchwork panels side by side and measure across the combined widths. If it measures 23" (58.4cm) then go ahead and sew the panels together. If it doesn't, then make a third unit or cut a strip of fabric or piece a strip of patchwork using smaller scraps to make up the required size.

6 Sew the units together and make sure that your patchwork panel measures at least 22 x 22" (55.9 x 55.9cm). If you want to give your work even more of a boro look then cut smaller squares, 3–4" (7.6–10.2cm) in size, and layer them on top of your patchwork. Sew into place with small running stitches approximately ¼" (6mm) in from the raw edges.

7 Give the patchwork top a good press and then layer it with quilt batting and plain cotton or calico backing fabric to make a quilt sandwich. Hold the layers together with curved safety pins or quilt basting spray.

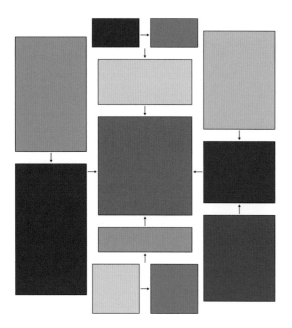

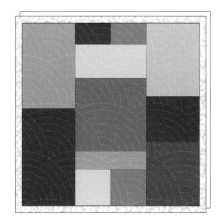

8 Quilt your pillow front as desired.

9 Trim the quilted pillow front to 20½ x 20½" (52 x 52cm) and set aside.

10 Make the envelope back. Cut two panels of fabric each 20½ x 15½" (52 x 39.3cm). Press a double ½" (13mm) hem along one of the 20½" (52cm) sides on both panels. Topstitch the hem with matching thread. Set aside.

11 Make the piping cord following the instructions on page 53. You will need to make 90" (228.6cm) of covered piping cord using 1½" (3.8cm) strips of fabric sewn end to end with diagonal seams. Make a knot in one end of the piping cord to stop it slipping through the fabric as you sew. Wrap the fabric strip around the piping cord and bring the raw edges together. Use a zipper foot on your sewing machine to sew near to the piping cord – but not quite as near as you can possibly get. That comes later!

12 Pin the prepared piping cord around the pillow front, matching raw edges of the covered cord with the raw edges of the pillow front. At the corners snip into the fabric covering the cord approximately ½" (13mm) from the end to allow you to bend it around the corner. When you get back to the start carefully cross the covered cord starting point, finish off the edge and pin in place.

13 Sew the covered cord to the pillow front using a zipper foot and following the first line of sewing.

14 Lay the envelope backing pieces over the pillow front, right sides together. Pin carefully.

15 Sew around the edge of the pillow, butting the zipper foot right up against the piping cord and with the machine needle as far to the left as possible. Sew all around the pillow front.

16 Turn the pillow through to the right side and check your work. If you haven't got quite close enough to the piping cord in places you can turn it back to the wrong side and have another go. When you are happy with the result, turn your work back through to the wrong side and zigzag over the raw edges to neaten them.

17 Turn the pillow through to the right side and insert your cushion pad.

18 I like to hover a steam iron over the front and back of a pillow to take any little creases out before plumping and setting it on the sofa in pride of place!

If you want to use this technique for larger pieces such as the quilted Haori Jacket, work on large squares of rectangles of a similar size. Join the 22 x 22" (55.9 x 55.9cm) squares together to make a large enough piece of 'fabric' and then layer and quilt as instructed in the pattern.

Patchwork and Quilted Slippers

INTERMEDIATE

My unisex Patchwork and Quilted Slippers can be made very simply with quilted fabric. You can make patchwork especially, or use leftover units from other projects. They are quick to make, stylish and comfortable and very giftable too! Make them in your favourite fabric combination or to match a quilt. Why not make a pair for every season?

The pattern fits most people's feet but if you want to scale the pattern up or down by 10–15% you can do that on a photocopier, or just reduce or extend the pattern pieces by 1" (2.5cm) on all sides and increase the length of the binding a little. If in doubt, make a quick mock-up of the slippers in unquilted calico, check the fit and then make adjustments as needed.

PROJECT SIZE

One size fits most (approx 5-9 UK size)

· See pullout sheet for templates

YOU WILL NEED

· 2 fat quarters of coordinating fabric for the upper, upper sole and binding *or* one fat quarter for the upper sole and binding plus scraps or spare patchwork to make the patchwork upper (see project introduction)
· 1 fat quarter of fabric to line the uppers – plain cotton is fine
· Fusible foam such as Bosal In R Form or quilt batting
· Non-slip Utility Grip fabric from Bosal for the slipper soles
· Thread for piecing and quilting
· 1" (2.5cm) wide bias tape maker
· Template material

SKILLS USED

· Using templates
· Simple patchwork
· Layering and quilting
· Making and attaching bias binding

Let's make the slippers!

1   If you're making slippers with new fabric, layer one fat quarter of patterned outer fabric with batting or fusible foam and a cotton backing, then quilt as desired. I quilted narrow parallel lines approximately ½" (13mm) apart. From this fabric you can cut two uppers and one left and one right sole.

2   If you're making the patchwork version, sew your patchwork units together to make a piece approximately 18 x 21" (45.7 x 53cm). If you're making patchwork just for the slippers I think 1½ x 1½" (3.8 x 3.8cm) squares sewn together looks lovely and suits the scale of slippers. Small half square triangles look great too or you could even use orphan blocks. Layer the patchwork with fusible foam and plain cotton backing fabric and quilt. Cut out two uppers and one left and one right sole.

Continue overleaf...

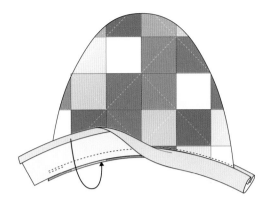

3   Cut a right and a left sole from the utility grip fabric and baste to the bottom of each quilted sole.

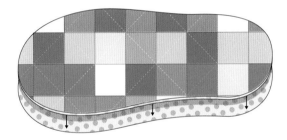

4   You could also just make and quilt enough fabric to make patchwork uppers and have plain quilted soles. So many choices!

5   Make around 75" (190.5cm) of bias binding. Cut 2" (5cm) wide strips of fabric on the bias and join with diagonal seams. Run the fabric through a 1" (2.5cm) wide tape maker.

6   Bind the upper edge of each of the uppers. Sew the binding to the front of the upper, raw edges aligned, then flip the binding to the back and sew by hand or machine.

7   Neaten one end of the remaining bias tape by folding a ½" (13mm) hem and pressing. Open out the binding and, starting at the inside edge of the slipper, sew the binding all around the sole, including where the upper joins the sole. You might want to pin carefully around the top and heel and ease the binding around the curve to get a neat finish. When you get back to the start overlap the binding by 1" (2.5cm) and snip off.

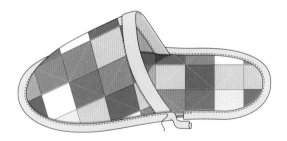

8   Flip the folded edge of the binding over the raw edge of the slipper and neatly glue or baste the binding. Either hand sew the binding in place or machine sew from the top of the slipper, ⅛" (3mm) inside the binding, which gives a smart and professional finish. Make the second slipper in exactly the same way.

9   Slippers on. Feet up. Relax!

She Sells Seashells Cushion

INTERMEDIATE

Bring a little of the seashore into your home with my quick and easy shell and starfish cushion. Combine simple appliqué starfish with easy patchwork and mother-of-pearl buttons to create a gorgeous detailed pillow that will have you dreaming of rockpooling! I like to use feather-filled cambric pads for squashy, plump and generously padded cushions.

PROJECT SIZE

Finished cushion 14 x 18" (35.6 x 45.7cm)

- See pullout sheet for templates

YOU WILL NEED

- Two 8½ x 8½" (21.6 x 21.6cm) squares of fabric for the starfish appliqués – I used a golden and a mottled brown and cream batik
- Two 8½ x 8½" (21.6 x 21.6cm) squares of fabric for the starfish backgrounds – I used two light blue prints
- 1 fat quarter of fabric for the narrow bands and binding – I used a tan stripe
- One 5 x 8½" (12.7 x 21.6cm) strip of fabric for the button bands – I used a medium brown spotted fabric
- 1 fat quarter of fabric for the outer border – I used a mock patchwork indigo/brown and blue print
- 2 fat quarters of fabric for the envelope back. I used two different Japanese-style prints
- 6 large flat mother-of-pearl buttons
- 4 medium flat mother-of-pearl buttons
- 8½ x 17" (21.6cm x 43.1cm) piece lightweight fusible interfacing (the kind used in dressmaking)
- Threads to match your appliqué fabrics, for piecing and for quilting
- 18 x 20" (45.7 x 50.8cm) quilt batting

- 18 x 20" (45.7 x 50.8cm) muslin or soft calico for the cushion front backing
- 14 x 18" (35.6 x 45.7cm) cushion pad (pillow form)
- Template material

SKILLS USED

- Using templates
- Turned edge appliqué
- Piecing
- Double-fold binding
- Making an envelope backing
- Basting
- Sewing buttons

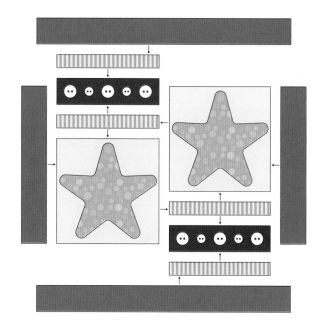

Continue overleaf...

Let's make the cushion!

Use a ¼" (6mm) seam allowance throughout.

1   Make a template of the starfish using either thin card or template plastic. Transfer the shape to the wrong side of your starfish fabrics but do not cut the starfish out.

2   Layer the right side of one starfish fabric with an 8½ x 8½" (21.6 x 21.6cm) square of interfacing, placing the right side of the fabric against the glue side of the interfacing. Pin the fabrics together, but on no account iron!

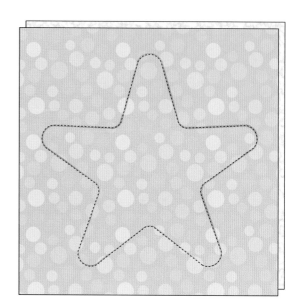

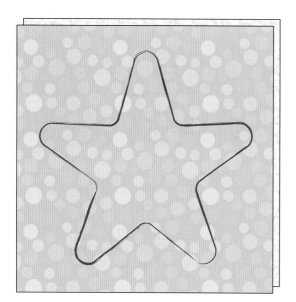

3   Using a short (2.0) stitch length on your machine sew around the starfish shape, sewing directly on your traced line. Turn your work carefully at the inner and outer curves to create smooth lines.

4   Trim the fabric and interfacing very close to the stitched line – somewhere between ¼" (6mm) and ⅛" (3mm). Clip into the inner curves at ⅛" (3mm) intervals. Clip close to the stitching line but not through it.

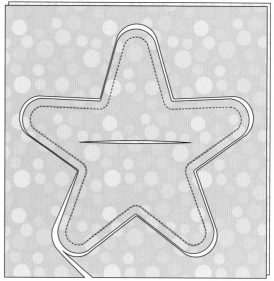

Continue overleaf...

5   Carefully cut a slip in the back of the
    interfacing and turn the arms of the starfish
    through to the right side. Use a chopstick or
    turning tool to help you and be careful not
    to push too hard. Interfacing is very delicate!

6   Carefully shape the starfish and finger press
    the edges, but do not iron.

7   Take one 8½ x 8½" (21.6 x 21.6cm) square of
    appliqué background fabric and centre the
    prepared starfish appliqué on it ensuring
    there is at least ¼" (6mm) space on all sides.

8   Iron the starfish in place. The interfacing
    glue will attach it to the background square.

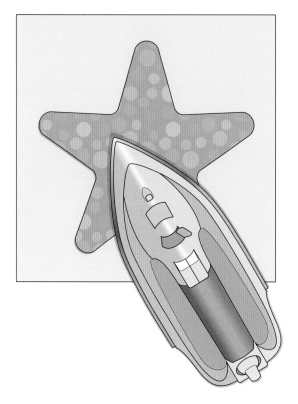

9 Use a blanket stitch or small zigzag and matching thread on your sewing machine and carefully sew around the appliqué. Make two.

10 Cut four 1½ x 8½" (3.8 x 21.6cm) narrow strips from your striped fabric for the narrow bands. Cut four 2½" x 21" (6.4 x 53cm) strips for the binding and set aside.

11 Cut two 2½ x 8½" (6.4 x 21.6cm) rectangles from the brown spot fabric for the button bands. Sew a narrow 1½" (3.8cm) strip to either side of the button bands and press. Make two.

12 Sew a pieced button band to the top of one starfish appliqué and the bottom of the other. Press. Join the two starfish panels together to create a 12½ x 16½" (31.7 x 41.9cm) centre panel.

13 From your outer border fabric cut four 2½" (6.4cm) strips – two 12½" (31.7cm) long and two 20½" (52cm) long.

14 Sew the short side borders on first and press, then add the long top and bottom borders. Give everything a final press.

15 Layer your cushion front with batting and calico or muslin backing to make a quilt sandwich and quilt as desired. I quilted my cushion front with a pattern called 'clamshells'. I couldn't resist the sea connection! After quilting add decorative buttons to the button bands, I used a mixture of small and large mother of pearl buttons.

16 Trim the quilted panel to 15½ x 19½" (39.3 x 49.5cm), trimming just a little off each side to square up your work.

17 Make the cushion back next. From each of your two backing fat quarters cut a 15½" x 15½" (39.3 x 39.3cm) square. Turn a double ½" (13mm) hem down one side of each and press, then topstitch in place using a slighter longer stitch than usual.

18 Layer the two backing pieces on the back of the cushion front, with the right side of the hemmed edges uppermost and crossing in the middle. Pin the backing in place and baste by hand or machine.

19 Join the four 2½" (6.4cm) binding strips together using straight or diagonal seams and then press in half lengthwise, wrong sides together, to create the double-fold binding. Neaten one end by turning and pressing a ½" (13mm) hem.

20 Attach your binding to the cushion front following the directions for binding a quilt on page 45. Mitre the corners carefully. Turn the binding to the back and slip stitch in place by hand or sew 'in the ditch' from the front to attach the binding by machine.

21 Insert your cushion pad and plump generously!

The Dower House

in *Summer*

Summertime in the country is all about endless sunny days, bright blue skies and the beauty of a cottage garden. Early mornings are filled with sunlight and the promise of another glorious day with the windows wide open, letting in the light and the scent of the garden. Days are spent among roses in full bloom and pergolas covered in sweet peas, immersed in the heady mix of floral scents and the sound of bees collecting pollen. Walk along the village high street to a grand old house, dripping with wisteria. You have arrived at the Dower House.

At the Dower House, nestled at the very heart of the village, a romantic mix of pretty, floral and very feminine projects awaits. Inspired by the beauty of an English country garden and the spectacular old houses you sometimes find in villages, where faded grandeur finds new life with softly hued vintage florals, gingham and fresh white cotton. My Bloom Where You Are Planted Quilt brings the beauty of the garden into the bedroom, where deep raspberry and pink florals jostle with apple green and soft greys for a sumptuous and romantic quilt you'll love forever. Little padded hearts made with scraps adorn the bedknobs and windows and a Crazy Patchwork Cushion provides a comfortable place to sit and read in the shade. An afternoon in the garden, a picnic or high tea needs the perfect quilt and my Tea with Jane Quilt and Hand-Embroidered Cushion make the perfect partners for an elegant afternoon. If you want to be surrounded by flowers look no further than my Ring-A-Roses Quilt. Elegant rings are smothered with appliqué flowers in colours that will make it forever summer in your home.

Romantic *Country* Style

Romantic country decor takes its inspiration from the beauty of a cottage garden and times past. Shabby chic interiors often blend crisp white walls and white-painted wooden furniture with soft and pretty fabrics, heirloom florals, crisp linens, lace and ticking stripes mixed with vintage buttons, trims and other nods to a romantic past. Tables are adorned with tablecloths, hand stitched by ladies long past, and bedecked with ornate hairbrushes, silver-framed photographs and other small trinkets. The look is grand but feminine, stately but homely too.

Colour inspiration is wide when it comes to a romantic country interior. Just look at a traditional cottage garden and your palette is right there! I've been inspired by the colours of old roses, sweet peas, lilacs and wisteria, hollyhocks, delphiniums and carnations – all the old-fashioned favourites, softly bright and beautifully shaded, from deeply hued tightly packed buds to pale overblown blooms. Lots of green in leafy shades adds a beautiful contrast to the floral colours. For neutrals and background colours, crisp white works beautifully with anything brightly pastel and will really make the colours pop. If you're using more antique floral tones then keep things looking aged and vintage by using a warmer cream or tan.

To get the Romantic look for your quilts and sewn projects, use my 'Rule of Five Fabrics'. Take a large-scale print – in this case choose fabrics with large vintage-style florals. Then a medium-scale print with flower buds or leaves scattered across the fabric perhaps. Choose a small-scale print in a geometric or shirting style of fabric. Next, go for polka dot. This classic style fits the romantic theme perfectly. Finally, pick a striped fabric. Look for a floral stripe, mattress ticking or tea-towel stripe, which gives a beautiful nod to heritage and vintage textiles. Romantic country projects are the perfect home for trims, lace and buttons you have saved or for embellishing with embroidery or hand-stitched details.

Bloom Where You Are Planted Quilt

INTERMEDIATE

Bloom Where You Are Planted is a call to find joy in whatever situation one happens to be in... to celebrate the present and enjoy the moment. If that moment happens to be spent in a beautiful country garden, so much the better! This quilt features a variation on the traditional 'Dresden Plate' block, the blades of which remind me of flower petals. I've used a whole bunch of pretty floral fabrics in shades of dove grey, apple green and raspberry pink to make a quilt which is pretty, soft and feminine. The little chequerboard blocks corral the floral elements and help to create a pleasing sense of order.

PROJECT SIZE

Finished quilt 65 x 65" (165.1 x 165.1cm)
24 x block size 9 x 9" (22.9 x 22.9cm)
- See pullout sheet for templates

YOU WILL NEED

- 4 metres white on white (WOW) print background fabric
- 8 fat quarters of assorted soft grey prints
- 8 fat quarters of assorted apple green prints
- 10 fat quarters of assorted pink prints
- 6 fat quarters of assorted red and deep raspberry pink prints
- ¼ metre warm tan gingham for the inner border
- 1 metre raspberry pink floral border fabric
- 1 metre light fusible interfacing for the appliqué circles
- 71 x 71" (180.3 x 180.3cm) quilt batting
- 71 x 71" (180.3 x 180.3cm) backing fabric
- ½ metre apple-green small check fabric for the binding
- Thread for piecing, appliqué and quilting
- Template material

SKILLS USED

- Patchwork
- Trimming units to size
- Machine or hand appliqué
- Faced appliqué
- Joining strips with a diagonal seam
- Adding borders to a quilt
- Layering and quilting
- Adding binding to a quilt

Continue overleaf...

Let's make the quilt!

Make the Dresden quarter blocks first. Make a template of the Dresden Tumbler shape from either template plastic or freezer paper.

1 From your WOW background fabric cut a total of 24 background blocks, each 9½ x 9½" (24.1 x 24.1cm).

2 Make the Dresden Blades. From assorted pink, soft green and soft grey prints cut a total of 120 Dresden Tumblers. From one 5" (12.7cm) x width of fat quarter strip you can cut eight tumblers.

3 Fold a tumbler shape in half lengthwise, right sides together, and finger press. Sew across the folded top of the tumbler with a ¼" (6mm) seam allowance. Clip the folded point close to the stitching line then turn the seam through to the right side. Centre the seam down the centre back of the tumbler, using your press line as a guide. Lay the now pointed end of the tumbler flat on an ironing board and press the Dresden Blade flat. Make a total of 120 Dresden Blades and then sew them together in sets of five assorted blades. Sew from the raw thinner end up to the base of the point and backstitch to secure.

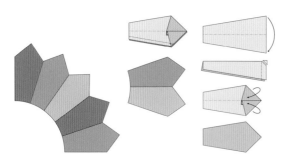

4 Appliqué the quarter blocks to the 9½ x 9½" (24.1 x 24.1cm) background squares.

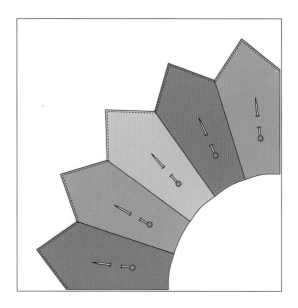

5 Trace 24 quarter circles onto light fusible interfacing then use my faced appliqué technique (see page 36) to prepare 24 quarter circles for appliqué using a variety of red and deep raspberry pink prints.

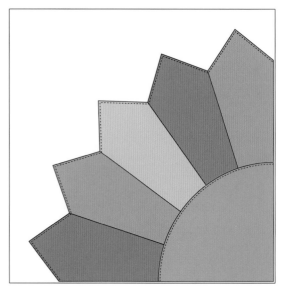

Appliqué the quarter circles over the raw lower edges of the Dresden blocks and baste the straight sides close to the raw edges.

6 Make the checkerboard and nine-patch sections next. From assorted soft grey print fat quarters cut a total of 15 strips, each 1½" (3.8cm) x width of fat quarter. From WOW background fabric cut a total of 12 strips, each 1½" (3.8cm) x width of fabric. Make six strip sets of grey/white/grey and three strip sets of white/grey/white using up all your strips. Cut fourteen 1½" (3.8cm) wide segments from each of the strip sets.

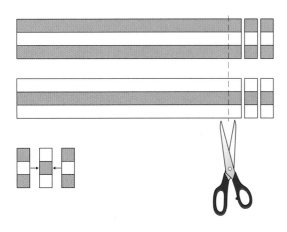

7 Combine the segments to make 36 grey-and-white nine-patch blocks, each measuring 3½" x 3½" (8.9 x 8.9cm) at this stage.

8 From assorted pink print fat quarters cut a total of nine 1½" (3.8cm) x width of fat quarter strips. From your WOW background print also cut a total of nine strips each 1½" (3.8cm) x width of fat quarter. Sew three strip sets of pink/white/pink and three strip sets of white/pink/white. Cut fourteen segments each 1½" (3.8cm) wide from each strip set.

9 Combine 18 segments to make a checkerboard section 3½" (8.9cm) wide by 18½" (47cm) long. Make four in total.

10 Make the half square triangles (HSTs) next. From assorted pink prints cut a total of 12 pink squares each 4 x 4" (10.2 x 10.2cm), from assorted green prints cut a total of eight squares each 4 x 4" (10.2 x 10.2cm) and from WOW background fabric cut a total of 20 squares each 4 x 4" (10.2 x 10.2cm).

11 Pair a pink and a WOW square, right sides together, and mark the diagonal lightly in pencil. Sew ¼" (6mm) either side of this line and then cut through the pencil line to yield two HST units. Press the unit with the seam allowance pressed towards the dark fabric. Trim the unit to 3½" x 3½" (8.9 x 8.9cm), making sure that the diagonal is kept from corner to corner. Make a total of 24 pink/white HSTs and 16 green/white HSTs, each 3½" x 3½" (8.9 x 8.9cm) at this stage.

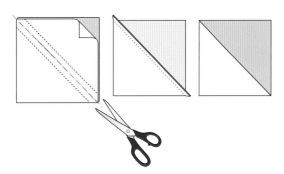

12 Cut eight assorted green squares each 3⅞ x 3⅞" (9.8 x 9.8cm). Cut each square once on the diagonal to yield a total of 16 HSTs. Cut 12 WOW squares at 3½ x 3½" (8.9 x 8.9cm) and four red/pink 3½ x 3½" (8.9 x 8.9cm) squares.

Continue overleaf...

13 Sew two green 3⅞" (9.8cm) triangles to two adjacent sides of a grey/white nine-patch unit. Press the seams towards the triangles. Make eight.

14 Use the Corner Trimming template to cut the corner off eight of the Dresden quarter blocks. Sew the nine-patch/green triangle units to replace these trimmed corners.

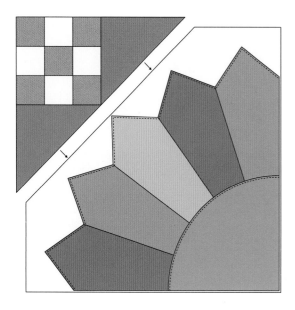

15 Lay out your blocks and pieced units following the assembly diagram above. Sew the units and blocks together. The quilt should measure 54½ x 54½" (138 x 138.4cm) at this point.

16 Add the inner border next. From warm tan gingham cut a total of six strips each 1½" (3.8cm) x width of fabric and join end to end with diagonal seams. From this strip cut two border pieces each 1½ x 54½" (3.8 x 138.4cm) and two border strips each 1½ x 56½" (3.8 x 143.5cm). Sew the shorter border strips to the shorter sides of the quilt and press towards the border. Sew the

remaining two longer border strips to the last two sides and press as before. Quilt now measures 56½ x 56½" (143.5 x 143.5cm).

17 From raspberry floral print border fabric cut six strips each 5" (12.7cm) x width of fabric and join end to end with straight seams to make a long strip. From this strip cut two border pieces each 5 x 56½" (12.7 x 143.5cm) and two strips each 5 x 65½" (12.7 x 166.3cm).

18 Sew the shorter borders to two opposite sides of the quilt and press towards the wide border. Add the longer border strips to the remaining sides and press. Quilt now measures 65½ x 65½" (166.3 x 166.3cm).

19 Layer your quilt top with batting and backing and baste together.

20 Quilt as desired. I quilted mine with swirling hearts. It's such a romantic quilt and it deserved a suitably heartfelt quilting pattern!

21 Trim the batting and backing even with the quilt top.

22 From your green check binding fabric cut seven strips each 2½" (6.4cm) x width of fabric and join end to end with diagonal seams. Bind the quilt and add a label to the back.

23 Your beautiful quilt is finished and will continue to bloom, come rain or shine!

Tea with Jane Quilt

BEGINNER/
INTERMEDIATE

Tea with Jane is a log cabin-like block that features thick 'logs' of beautiful soft coral, peach and pink florals and it's accented with thin 'logs' of warm tan. The block and indeed the quilt was inspired by afternoon tea with a friend, surrounded by the most incredible topiary – including a maze. I was captivated by the beautiful floral borders, edged with low hedges and pathways, and couldn't wait to make a start on my very own fabric version!

PROJECT SIZE

Finished quilt 77 x 77" x (195.6 x 195.6cm)
Block size 15 x 15" (38.1 x 38.1cm)
Number of blocks 16

YOU WILL NEED

- At least 4 metres or 16 fat quarters of fabric for the thick logs, but add more for extra variety or use the fat quarters as a base and then add extras from your scraps. You could also use a jelly roll or strip roll of forty 2½" (6.4cm) strips
- Fabric for the large squares. If you're using fat quarters for the thick logs then you'll have enough fabric to cut the squares too. If you want to feature one print throughout for the squares, you'll need ¾ metre
- 2½ metres fabric for the thin logs and sashings
- 1 fat quarter of fabric for the cornerstones if you want to use a different fabric, or you could use scraps left over from the blocks or sashings
- 1½ metres fabric for the outer border
- 83 x 83" (210.8 x 210.8cm) backing fabric
- 83 x 83" (210.8 x 210.8cm) quilt batting
- Threads for piecing and quilting

SKILLS USED

- Patchwork piecing
- Adding sashing and cornerstones
- Adding a simple border
- Layering and quilting
- Joining fabrics with a diagonal seam
- Adding a double-fold binding

How to cut and organise your fabrics

There are different strategies for getting the best from your fabrics. I would cut one of each of the block pieces from each fat quarter, one of every size of thick log, then mix and match the thick logs across all of your chosen fabrics. Do a full set from one fabric. Repeat this process with your other fat quarters and then mix and match them as you make the blocks.

For simplicity, I list the cutting instructions for one block in the order you will piece it (on page 109). The 'main fabric' refers to the large squares and all the thick logs, which are made out of patterned fat quarter fabric. The 'contrast fabric' refers to the thin logs and sashings – in my quilt, this is the tan stripe.

The large squares are 6½ x 6½" (16.5 x 16.5cm), so big enough but not huge. A small or medium-scale print will look good here, but if you have large-scale prints (or even one fabric repeated throughout) then it's a really good place to show them off! If you prefer you could piece this 6½ x 6½" (16.5 x 16.5cm)

Continue overleaf...

square: a four-patch made of four 3½ x 3½" (8.9 x 8.9cm) squares; or a nine-patch made with nine 2½ x 2½" (6.4 x 6.4cm) squares. You could even make the 6" x 6" (15.2 x 15.2cm) finished star blocks from the Sky Full of Stars Quilt (see page 138) and use them in place of the large squares.

I think it's best to use a solid, plain, tone-on-tone or hand-dyed batik for the thin logs. I've used a subtle stripe for mine and it adds a lovely contrast to the florals even though the colours are quite close.

For the thick logs you can use jelly roll strips as the strips required for the thick logs are cut at 2½" (6.4cm), but this pattern is perfectly compatible with fat quarters or you could use yardage, scraps, even layer cake squares for the shorter logs. Remember this is patchwork, so what about piecing shorter lengths of fabric to make the longer logs? I know this won't appeal to everyone but I'm just sowing the seed in your head. It's OK to piece!

Sashing The blocks are sashed. These sashings are the same fabric and the same width as the thin logs, which helps to create the 'maze' appearance.

Cornerstones I have placed cornerstones at the intersections of the sashings. Even when the sashings and the cornerstones are the same fabric I prefer to include cornerstones; you don't really see them, but they help to line everything up perfectly. There is nothing more annoying than wonky sashings and blocks in my humble opinion! Why not use the cornerstones to your advantage and add an extra pop of colour? Use a contrast, accent or toning colour and make your quilt a hit!

Binding This can be a final frame or border of sorts in a contrast colour, or you can make the binding disappear by using the same fabric as your final border. I use 2½" (6.4cm) folded strips of binding fabric to make double-fold binding (see page 45). It's strong, durable and looks great.

One 6½ x 6½" (16.5 x 16.5cm) square (main fabric)

Thin log 'round'

One 1½ x 6½" (3.8 x 16.5cm) (contrast)
One 1½ x 7½" (3.8 x 19cm) (contrast)

Thick log 'round'

One 2½ x 7½" (6.4 x 19cm) (main)
One 2½ x 9½" (6.4 x 24.1cm) (main)

Thin log 'round'

One 1½ x 9½" (3.8 x 24.1cm) (contrast)
One 1½ x 10½" (3.8 x 26.7cm) (contrast)

Thick log 'round'

One 2½ x 10½" (6.4 x 26.7cm) (main)
One 2½ x 12½" (6.4 x 31.7cm) (main)

Thin log 'round'

One 1½ x 12½" (3.8 x 31.7cm) (contrast)
One 1½ x 13½" (3.8 x 34.3cm) (contrast)

Thick log 'round'

One 2½ x 13½" (6.4 x 34.3cm) (main)
One 2½ x 15½" (6.4 x 39.3cm) (main)

Each block is made up of one large square, thin logs and thick logs.

Continue overleaf...

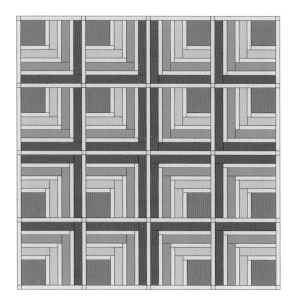

Let's make the quilt!

Use a ¼" (6mm) seam allowance throughout. Check your seam allowance carefully before you begin. This is a straightforward block and a strikingly beautiful and simple quilt, but you need to be accurate in your cutting and piecing. Don't be tempted to trim the ends of strips off if they don't quite fit, or you won't end up with 15 x 15" (38.1 x 38.1cm) finished blocks and nothing will fit together as it should.

1   Start with your 6½ x 6½" (16.5 x 16.5cm) square. If it's cut out of a directional fabric, think about its orientation in the quilt and add the thin and thick logs to the correct sides. Otherwise sew the 1½ x 6½" (3.8 x 16.5cm) strip of contrast fabric to one side. We will call this the A side. Press the seam towards the large square. Sew the 1½ x 7½" (3.8 x 19cm) contrast strip to an adjacent side. We will call this side B. Press the seam allowance towards the large square.

2   Sew a 2½ x 7½" (6.4 x 19cm) strip of main fabric to side A and press towards the thick log. Sew the 2½ x 9½" (6.4 x 24.1cm) strip to side B and again press the seam allowance towards the thick log.

3   Continue adding rounds in this way working through all your strips. Always add the shorter of the pair to side A and the longer of the pair to side B. Your block should measure 15 x 15" (38.1 x 38.1cm).

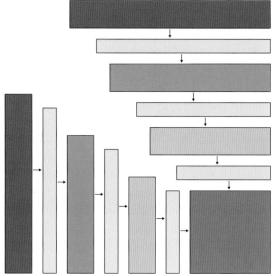

4   Make a total of 16 blocks. If fabric and time allow, make a couple of extra blocks, especially if you are using scraps. Extra blocks are so useful when it comes time to setting the blocks together. If you find that you have one or two blocks that won't 'play nicely' with the others, you can turn them into matching cushions.

5   Lay your blocks out in four rows of four blocks. I grouped four blocks in the centre to form a cross and then echoed the direction of the block out towards the corners. There

are lots of setting possibilities with this quilt, so take time to try different layouts, take lots of photographs and pick the formation you love best.

6 Now add the sashings and the cornerstones. Each sashing piece is 1½ x 15½" (3.8 x 39.3cm). You'll need to cut 40 sashing strips. Also cut 25 cornerstones, each 1½ x 1½" (3.8 x 3.8cm). I've used a different fabric to the sashing, but it's a close match. You could use scraps from the blocks if you prefer.

7 I like to lay out my blocks on the floor with the sashing and cornerstones placed where they will be sewn. It's a bit of bending and stretching but sometimes it's the only exercise I get and it keeps me organised!

8 Working in vertical rows, sew sashing to the top and bottom edges of a block and press the seams towards the sashing strip. Miss the next block out and repeat the sashings on the top and bottom edges of the third block in the vertical column. On the fourth and final block, sew sashing to the bottom edge only. Sew the entire row together, pressing seam allowances towards the sashing each time. Repeat this process for all four vertical columns in the quilt.

9 Now sew cornerstones and sashing strips together; first a cornerstone, then a sashing strip. Repeat until the full sashing column is made. Press the seam allowances towards the sashing. Make five of these columns. Sew the sashing columns and the block columns together, carefully matching the seam intersections and the cornerstones.

10 Your quilt centre should measure 65½ x 65½" (166.3 x 166.3cm).

11 From your border print fabric cut seven strips each 6½" (16.5cm) x width of fabric (42"/106.7cm). Sew these strips end to end and press the seams open. From this length cut two border strips each 65½" (166.3cm) long and two 77½" (196.9cm) long.

12 Sew the shorter border strips to the two shorter sides and press the seam allowances towards the border. Sew the longer border strips to the remaining two sides and again press the seam allowances towards the borders. Your quilt top should now measure 77½ x 77½" (196.9 x 196.9cm).

13 Give the top a good press and trim any loose threads.

14 Layer the quilt top with backing and batting and quilt as desired. I quilted loose, flowing feathers and swirls all over the top. A simple cross-hatch design would look great too!

15 Trim the edges of the quilt even with the top.

16 Cut eight strips of binding each 2½" (6.4cm) x width of fabric and join with diagonal seams. Use the strips to bind the edge of the quilt using the double-fold method (see page 45). Now label your quilt.

17 If you want to use one block to make a cushion add a simple 3" (7.6cm) cut border to all sides, then layer and quilt. You could add covered piping cord to the edges (see page 53) or a bound edge as on the She Sells Seashells Cushion (see page 90). The finished cushion will be 20 x 20" (50.8 x 50.8cm) square.

18 It's time for tea in the garden!

Crazy Patchwork Cushion

BEGINNER/
INTERMEDIATE

The Crazy Patchwork is a versatile and fun way to use up scraps of fabric or to make a coordinating cushion to go with a larger quilt – the perfect use for all those oddments left at the end of making. You can use four small blocks to make a cushion, one block plus borders to make different kind of cushion or use a combination to make a beautiful quilt (see box on page 116). The choice is yours!

PROJECT SIZE
Finished cushion 16 x 16" (40 x 40cm) or
18 x 18" (45.7 x 45.7cm)

YOU WILL NEED
· Assorted scraps of fabrics for the patchwork. Odd shapes and sizes are perfect for this project!
· One 11 x 11" (28 x 28cm) square plain cotton fabric per block you want to make, in a light colour for the foundation
· Fabrics for the borders, if using
· 20 x 20" (50.8 x 50.8cm) quilt batting
· 20 x 20" (50.8 x 50.8cm) backing fabric in a light plain colour
· Quilt basting spray or curved safety pins
· 2 metres cotton piping cord, ⅜" (1cm) diameter
· ¼ metre fabric for covering the piping cord
· ½ metre coordinating fabric for the cushion back
· 16 x 16" (40 x 40cm) or 18" x 18" (45.7 x 45.7cm) cushion pad (pillow form)
· Sewing thread

SKILLS USED
· Crazy patchwork sewn to a foundation
· Adding borders
· Layering and quilting
· Making covered piping cord
· Making an envelope backing

Let's make the cushion!

1   First make the crazy patchwork squares. Each square will be 9 x 9" (22.9 x 22.9cm). Cut a 11 x 11" foundation square of plain fabric. You will sew the crazy patches directly to this foundation.

2   Cut your first piece for the patchwork. This needs to be a four- or five-sided shape. It doesn't have to be accurate, but make sure the sides are straight. I often start with an irregular hexagon, which gives me lots of scope for adding patches to the five sides.

3   Place this first patch right side up onto the foundation square, somewhere near the middle. Cut a second patch of scrap fabric. A rough rectangle is a good starting point. It needs to be as long as one of the sides of the first patch. Layer the pieces right sides together and sew together through the foundation, then open the patches and press them.

Continue overleaf...

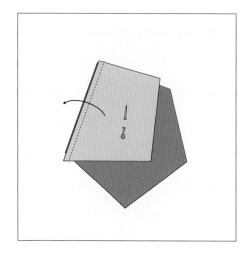

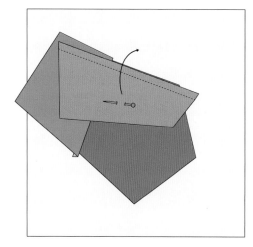

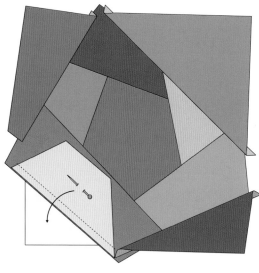

4 Trim the edges of your first two patches so that they are even and then cut a patch to fit the next side of the first shape. Keep adding patches until the first patch is surrounded, then add more patches to fill the rest of the foundation, working out from the centre patch.

5 As you get nearer to the outer edges you might find that your patches need to be larger than the available fabric scraps. This isn't a problem – simply sew two or three smaller pieces of fabric together and then trim to the required size. This will only add beautiful variety and will put a little dent into your scrap pile.

6 Once the foundation is generously covered carefully trim it back to 9½" x 9½" (24.1 x 24.1cm). If you're making the 18" x 18" (45.7 x 45.7cm) finished cushion you'll need a total of four 9½" x 9½" (24.1 x 24.1cm) square blocks sewn together in two rows of two to make an 18½" x 18½" (47 x 47cm) square.

7 If you're making the smaller cushion you need one block to which you will add borders. The first round of borders is cut at 1" x 9½" (2.5 x 24.1cm) and 1" x 11" (2.5 x 28cm) – cut two of each. Sew this border on and press. The second border is 2½" x 11" (6.4 x 28cm) and 2½" x 15" (6.4 x 38.1cm) – cut two of each. Sew the border on and press. The final border strips are cut at 1½" (3.8cm), two 15" (38.1cm) long and two 17" (43.1cm) long.

8 Layer your cushion front with batting and the plain cotton backing fabric and baste them together with basting spray or curved safety pins. Quilt as desired. Trim a larger cushion front to 18½" x 18½" (47 x 47cm) and a smaller one to 16½" x 16½" (41.9 x 41.9cm).

Continue overleaf...

9   Make covered piping cord following the instructions on page 53. You will need enough to go around the perimeter of your cushion front plus 6" (15.2cm).

10 Pin then sew the piping cord to the cushion front. To turn the corners easily, snip into the fabric seam allowance of the piping cord approximately ½" (13mm) from the raw edge. This will create a 'bend' in the covered piping cord. I like to overlap the raw ends of my covered piping cord like a kiss where they would naturally join. There are fancier ways to join the ends together but this way works for me! Sew the piping cord to the cushion front using your zipper foot and sewing close the piping cord, but not as close as you can possibly get. That comes later.

11 Make the envelope back for the cushion following the instructions on page 52. For the larger cushion I cut my two panels each 15 x 18½" (38.1 x 47cm) and for the smaller cushion I cut my panels 12" x 16½" (30.5 x 41.9cm). Press then sew the inner hems to neaten and then pin the envelope backs to the cushion front, right sides together.

12 Sew around the perimeter of the cushion using your zipper foot and this time sewing as close as you possibly can to the piping cord.

13 Turn your cushion through to the right side and press. Insert your cushion pad and plump generously!

Make a Crazy Patchwork Quilt

If you want to use this technique for a quilt then I think you should! You can sew the crazy patchwork units edge to edge. Forty-eight blocks sewn edge to edge in a 6 x 8 arrangement would make a 48 x 64" (122 x 162.6cm) quilt – perfect as a wide border to top a bed or sofa. Alternatively you could sew four units together (as in the larger cushion) and then join these blocks with 2" (5cm) finished sashing. Twelve of these large blocks in a 3 x 4 arrangement with sashing would make a 62 x 82" (157.5 x 208.2cm) quilt. Add a 5" (12.7cm) border on all sides to make it 72 x 92" (183 x 233.7cm).

Crazy Scrap Hanging Hearts

CONFIDENT BEGINNER

My quilted hearts are a lovely make when you want to use up bits and bobs, add a little something to coordinate with a larger project or need a little gift in a hurry. One takes no time at all to make and you could easily turn them into bunting to string across the back of an iron bedstead. They also look lovely hung on doorknobs or as oversized key fobs. I've even made these to hang on the Christmas tree. Using leftover fabric from a larger project is ideal and then the hanging hearts will coordinate beautifully. See if you can stop at one!

PROJECT SIZE

Finished hearts approx 6 x 6"
(15.2 x 15.2cm)

· See pullout sheet for templates

YOU WILL NEED FOR EACH HEART

· Lots of assorted scraps of coordinating fabrics in small and medium-sized pieces. Don't worry if your pieces are odd shapes; they will work well in this project
· Narrow ribbon, lace and buttons (optional)
· 10 x 10" (25.4 x 25.4cm) plain cotton fabric in white or cream to form the patchwork foundation
· 10 x 10" (25.4 x 25.4cm) pretty backing fabric
· 10 x 10" (25.4 x 25.4cm) quilt batting
· Quilt basting spray or curved safety pins
· 9–14" (22.9–35.6cm) narrow ribbon or decorative cord for hanging
· Small quantity fibrefill/toy stuffing
· Hand sewing needle and thread
· Machine sewing thread
· Template material

SKILLS USED

· Using templates
· Simple crazy pieced patchwork
· Layering and quilting
· Adding a hanging loop
· Making a pieced backing
· Stuffing
· Sewing buttons

Let's make the hearts!

1   The crazy patchwork is made in a similar way to the Crazy Patchwork Cushion although I've included a few variations to ring the changes. You could practise the technique using other scraps first if you wanted, especially if your favourite fabrics are in short supply.

2   Cut your foundation fabric to approximately 10 x 10" (25.4 x 25.4cm) square. You will sew your scrap fabrics directly to the foundation.

3   Cut your first scrap into a four- or five-sided shape. It doesn't need to accurate – just make sure the sides are straight! Lay this first shape, right side up, somewhere near the centre of your foundation. Pin it in place.

Continue overleaf...

4   Cut a second scrap of fabric into a rough rectangle that is at least as long as one of the sides of piece number one. Lay it on top of your first patch, right sides together. Sew the seam right through the foundation using a ¼" (6mm) seam allowance. Press the two scrap patches apart.

5   Continue adding scrap patches to the remaining sides of the first patch. They don't all have to be rectangles; add a triangle on one or two sides or add your rectangles at more of a slanting angle to create more interest and a less log cabin style block.

6   As an alternative you can add patches to one side only. Piece to the outside of the block and then add patches to the remaining sides.

7   If the side you need to cover is rather large and your scraps rather small, don't be afraid to sew a couple of scraps together and trim the resulting fabric to the right size and shape before adding it to the foundation. Almost no scrap is too small to use if you use this technique!

8   For extra fancy crazy patchwork, layer some narrow ribbon or lace trim onto some of your patches and sew them in place by machine, sewing very close to either free edge.

9   Once you have generously covered the foundation square you can trim it to a neat 10" x 10" (25.4 x 25.4cm) square ready for quilting.

10 Once your patchwork is completed it's time to layer it with some quilt batting. There's no need to add any backing fabric at this stage. Quilt your patchwork as desired;

keep it simple with straight lines of quilting near your seamlines or sew an all-over design. You could even use embroidery floss and add decorative hand stitches. If you do this, it might be helpful to lightly mark the position of the heart template onto your patchwork and keep your embroidery designs within this line.

11 Make the backing for the heart by folding the backing square, right sides together, in half and then clip the tiniest sliver off the fold to create two rectangles. Keep them right sides together. Now sew the rectangle back together using a ¼" (6mm) seam allowance and leaving a 3" (7.6cm) gap in the centre of the seam for turning. Reinforce your stitching by sewing forwards and backwards several times before and after leaving the turning gap to prevent the seam 'popping' open when you stuff it. Press the whole seam open.

12 Make a template using the Hanging Heart template on the pullout sheet. There's no need to add a seam allowance. Mark around this template on the wrong side of the pieced backing. This line is your sewing line. I like to keep the open join near the centre of the heart and away from the inner or outer point of the heart where the extra seam allowance would add bulk.

13 Lay the pieced backing on the quilted patchwork, right sides together.

14 Fold the ribbon or cord that you are using to hang the heart and carefully insert it between the backing and the patchwork, with the loop facing down and the raw ends just hanging over the inner point of the heart. Pin in place.

Continue overleaf...

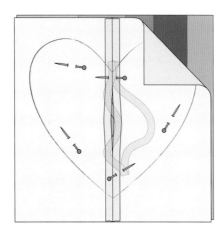

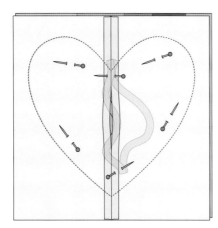

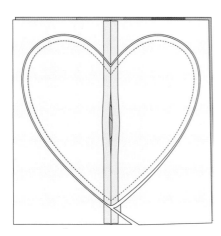

16 Using sharp scissors cut around the heart adding a narrow hem (less than ¼"/6mm) by eye. Snip down into the seam allowance at the inner point, cutting near to but not through the stitches.

17 Turn the heart through to the right side and carefully push the shape out neatly. Press.

18 Lightly stuff the heart with fibrefill or toy stuffing, using small amounts at a time and getting the stuffing into the upper curves and lower point first.

19 Use a hand sewing needle and thread to close the opening in the backing using small slip stitches or a ladder stitch.

20 Add decorative buttons or bows if desired.

21 You can make different kinds of crazy patchwork. Try sewing longer strips of varying widths to the foundation, either in a straight row or at an angle. If you are opting for the angled version start by drawing a pencil line on your foundation square at a 45 degree angle or simply layer your first strip from corner to corner and add your remaining strips to either side.

22 If you want to use your hearts to create padded bunting make them in exactly the same way but add a single piece of ribbon or cord rather than a loop. Using ready-made wide bias tape, insert the hanging cord or ribbon of each heart at regular distances along the tape, approximately 8" (20.3cm) apart. Pin the folded tape together and then machine sew very close to the open side of the tape to join and attach the hanging hearts in one step.

15 Sew around the heart, right on the drawn line, using a slightly shorter stitch than usual. Sew around the entire perimeter of the heart.

Hand-Embroidered Cushion

INTERMEDIATE

I love to find a cosy spot on a warm summer afternoon to sit and read a favourite book – but I also like to be comfortable and a plump cushion is just the thing! I love small projects with lots of detail in them. This cushion has it all; pretty patchwork, delightful hand embroidery, a sweet folded accent border, mother-of-pearl buttons and a smart piped edge.

The patchwork pinwheels have some lovely subtle detail in them. The cream side is made up of two different fabrics sewn together. a scrap-busting technique that creates little secondary pinwheels! Build your skills and create an heirloom to treasure.

PROJECT SIZE
Finished cushion 18 x 18" (45.7 x 45.7cm)
- See step five for embroidery design and template sheet for patterns

YOU WILL NEED
- Assorted strips of cream/ivory print fabrics; minimum eight strips 2½ x 20" (6.4 x 50.8cm)
- Pink prints and chocolate brown prints in 4½ x 4½" (11.4 x 11.4cm) squares. You need eight of each colour and 4-8 different prints in each colour
- 8 x 8" (20.3 x 20.3cm) background fabric for the embroidery
- 8 x 8" (20.3 x 20.3cm) light fusible woven interfacing
- Embroidery floss in mid-chestnut brown, deep chocolate brown and variegated pink
- Crewel needle and 6" (15.2cm) embroidery hoop
- 1 fat quarter of deep chocolate brown print for the folded accent border and the covered piping cord
- Four ¾" (19mm) and two ½" (13mm) mother-of-pearl buttons, or other decorative buttons to suit your project
- 2 metres cotton piping cord, ⅜" (1cm) diameter
- 21 x 21" (53 x 53cm) quilt batting

- 21 x 21" (53 x 53cm) plain cotton fabric to back the quilted cushion front
- ½ metre coordinating fabric for the envelope back
- 18 x 18" (45.7 x 45.7cm) cushion pad (pillow form)
- Small square up ruler (optional)
- Thread for piecing and quilting

SKILLS USED
- Strip piecing and easy patchwork
- Hand embroidery
- Making a folded accent border
- Layering and quilting
- Sewing buttons
- Making and adding covered piping cord
- Making an envelope back

Continue overleaf...

Let's make the cushion!

1 Make the strip pieced patchwork first. Take two 2½" (6.4cm) cream strips and sew them together, pressing the seam allowance open. This makes a strip pieced unit 4½ (11.4cm) wide. Make four units. Cut four 4½ x 4½" (11.4 x 11.4cm) squares from each of the strip sets to get a total of sixteen.

2 Pair one strip pieced cream square with a pink 4½ x 4½" (11.4 x 11.4cm) square and mark the diagonal on the back of the plain square lightly with pencil. Sew ¼" (6mm) either side of this line, cut on the drawn line and press the seam allowances towards the plain fabric to create two half square triangle (HST) units. Make a total of 32 HST units using all of the strip pieced units paired with either a pink or a brown plain square.

3 At the moment your HST units will be a little oversized. Use the square up ruler or your rotary ruler to trim the units to 3½ x 3½" (8.9 x 8.9cm). Make sure that the diagonal piecing line is lined up with the 45 degree line on your ruler when you trim.

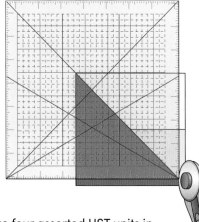

4 Take four assorted HST units in the pink/cream combination and arrange them in a pinwheel. Sew the units together and press the seams open. This helps to spread the bulk of the seam allowances across the block and helps to create more accurate, flatter patchwork. Make a total of four pink pinwheels and four chocolate brown pinwheels. Set aside.

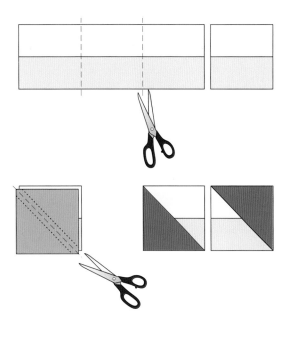

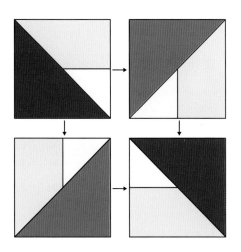

Continue overleaf...

5 Complete your embroidery next. Trace the Floral Wreath design (see page 205) onto your background square, centring the design carefully, then iron the fusible interfacing to the wrong side of the background square. Hoop your fabric and work the design using two strands of embroidery floss and a combination of backstitch and French knots (see page 51). I used chestnut brown for the hoop, dark chocolate brown for the leaves and a variegated pink floss for the circles and flowers. When the embroidery is complete carefully press your work from the reverse and then trim to 6½ x 6½" (16.5 x 16.5cm), making sure that the design is centred.

6 Add the folded accent border to your embroidery. From the chocolate brown accent fabric cut four strips each 1 x 7" (2.5 x 17.8cm) and fold each in half lengthwise, wrong sides together, and press. Line up one folded strip against one edge of your embroidery, long raw edges aligned and ¼" (6mm) of the folded strip hanging off each end. The fold should face inwards towards the embroidery. Now carefully baste the strip in place ⅛" (3mm) in from the

raw edge. Trim the overhang level with the block. Repeat on the remaining three sides, working in a clockwise direction. The block size remains unchanged; it should still measure 6½ x 6½" (16.5 x 16.5cm).

7 Arrange the pinwheel blocks and the embroidery to form the cushion front and sew the blocks into three rows. Press the seams open throughout.

8 Layer your cushion front with batting and backing and either spray baste or pin with curved safety pins. Quilt your cushion front. I quilted straight lines following the piecing and quilted ⅛" (3mm) away from the seams.

9 Sew buttons to two opposite corners of the embroidery.

10 Trim your batting and backing evenly with the cushion front.

11 Make the covered piping cord next. Follow the instructions on page 53 to make 2 metres of covered piping cord. Pin then baste the piping cord in place around the outside edge of the cushion.

12 Make the envelope back. You will need two panels from your backing fabric, each 15 x 18½" (38.1 x 47cm). Make and sew a double ½" (13mm) hem on one long edge of each panel, layer and sew the backing in place following the instructions on page 52.

13 It's worth overlocking or zigzag stitching the raw edges to make the cushion extra durable. Once this is done turn your cushion though to the right side, insert your pillow form and plump generously!

14 Grab a book, find a cosy nook and dream.

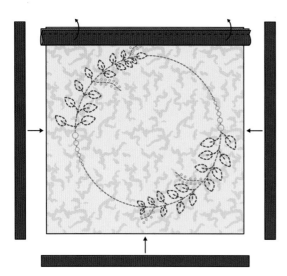

Ring-A-Roses Quilt

INTERMEDIATE

My Ring-A-Roses Quilt was inspired by the playground rhyme, 'Ring a ring-a-roses, a pocket full of posies', and happy childhood memories of our garden, filled in the summer with myriads of blooms. Interlocking rings of stems and leaves are adorned with overblown roses, buds and berries and the wide border perfectly corrals the blooms within. This is a very easy quilt to re-colour and would look stunning in blues and whites; reds, pinks and whites; or a whole rainbow of warm autumnal shades. Let this pattern bring out the gardener in you and create your own little piece of heaven!

PROJECT SIZE

Finished quilt 64 x 64" (162.6 x 162.6cm)

Block size 16 x 16" (40 x 40cm)

Number of blocks four full blocks and eight half blocks

· See pullout sheet for templates

YOU WILL NEED

· 2 metres white print or solid for the appliqué background
· 5 fat quarters of assorted greens for the stems and leaves
· 5 fat quarters of assorted blue prints for the leaves, flowers, buds and the scrappy binding
· 5 fat quarters of assorted peach and coral prints for the leaves, flowers, berries and buds
· 4 fat eighths of assorted yellow prints for the flowers, berries and buds
· 2½ metres large-scale yellow floral fabric for the border
· Threads for piecing and to match your appliqué fabrics
· 2 metres fusible appliqué webbing
· ⅜" (1cm) bias tape maker
· Fabric-safe glue pen
· Spray starch
· Template material

SKILLS USED

· Simple patchwork
· Fusible appliqué
· Using a bias binding tool
· Adding a simple border
· Layering and quilting
· Rounding the corners of a quilt
· Binding with bias binding

Continue overleaf...

Let's make the quilt!

Each full block is made up of four stems that curve from corner to corner. The half blocks feature one single curved stem and they are appliquéd first, then joined together to create a framework. Once the quilt is made you can do your own thing with the appliqués. Follow my version exactly or prepare a whole garden full of stems, leaves, berries and blossoms and create your very own fabric garden. To complement the curves and circles in the appliqué I have gently curved the corners of this quilt and bound the edge with binding cut on the bias. Do the same if you wish or keep the corners crisp and square.

1   Spray starch and press your green fabrics lightly to prepare them for making bias stems. Cut ¾" (19mm) wide strips of fabric on the bias and then run them through your bias tape maker to create the stems for your quilt. Most of the stems are pretty long, so cut your bias stems from the longest diagonal on your fat quarters. This will leave two large triangles at either side that you can use for leaves. You will need 24 stems total for the 'rings' and each stem needs to be 17" (43.1cm) long. You'll also need eight stems 15" (38.1cm) long plus four short pieces approximately 4" (10.2cm) long for the outer floral sprays, and for the centre motif four stems 13" (33cm) long and four stems 11" (28cm) long. Keep the stems in piles of the same length.

2   From your white background fabric cut four large squares each 16½ x 16½" (41.9 x 41.9cm), eight rectangles each 8½ x 16½" (21.6 x 41.9cm) and four squares each 8½ x 8½" (21.6 x 21.6cm).

3   Make the full blocks first. Use the stem placement guide (see below) to position the four stems and glue into place with a thin line of fabric-safe glue on the underside of each stem. Either sew the bias stems in place with a hand slip stitch or machine sew very close to the edge of the stem with a matching thread. Repeat to make four blocks.

4   Use the same technique to create eight half blocks. These have a single stem running from corner to corner, placed using the same template. Appliqué the stems in place as before.

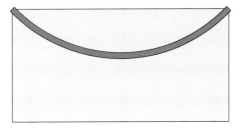

Continue overleaf...

5   Lay out your four full blocks, your eight half blocks and the plain corner squares, then sew the blocks together using a ¼" (6mm) seam allowance. Press all the seams open. Your quilt top should measure 48½ x 48½" (123.2 x 123.2cm) at this point.

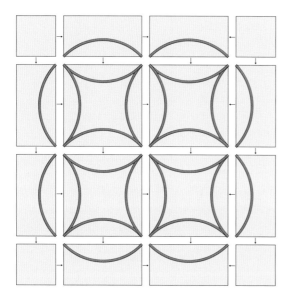

6   Using the quilt photographs as a guide, lay down your eight 15" (38.1cm) stems at the corners to create the outer swags. I added some shorter stems towards the ends of theses stems too, just before the circular buds. Glue the stems down and appliqué. Finally lay down the 13" (33cm) and 11" (28cm) stems, working outwards from the very centre of the quilt. Tuck the raw ends of the shorter stems under the longer ones and glue then appliqué into place.

7   Prepare your appliqué leaves, flowers, buds and berries. I like to cut templates from template plastic or thin card; it's much quicker to trace around a shape than to trace through paper. Prepare five large

flowers for the outer swags and centre motif and four smaller flowers for the inner motifs. Each flower also has a large and a slightly smaller circle for the centre, but feel free to mix this up. Arrange the flowers and fuse into place, then sew around the edges with a blanket or zigzag stitch. Prepare at least 72 leaves in various sizes and a wide variety of colours. Most of my leaves are set down in pairs but don't stick slavishly to this – it's not nature's way! Arrange your leaves and once you are happy with the placement and balance of colours fuse and appliqué into place. I used a machine blanket stitch but a zigzag works well too. Finally prepare at least 64 circles of various sizes for the buds and berries. Fuse the berries into place and sew around the edges.

8   Give your quilt top a press and trim any loose threads. Add the outer border. You will need to cut eight strips of fabric, each 8½" (21.6cm) x width of fabric. Join the strips together with a ¼" (6mm) seam allowance, then from this continuous length cut two strips each 8½ x 48½" (21.6 x 123.2cm) for the side borders and two strips each 8½ x 64½" (21.6 x 163.8cm) for the top and bottom borders. Sew the side borders to the quilt first and press the seams towards the border fabric. Then add the top and bottom borders and again press the seam allowances towards the borders. Your quilt should now measure 64½" x 64½" (163.8 x 163.8cm).

9   Layer your quilt top with batting and backing fabric cut at least 2" (5cm) or 3" (7.6cm) bigger on all sides. Quilt as desired. I did an all-over quilting motif of hearts and swirls, but you could echo quilt (echo quilting is when you quilt around the

Continue overleaf...

edge of a motif to create a ripple effect following the shape of appliqués several times like ripples on a pond) around each of the appliqué swags and then fill the background in with a meander or cross-hatching.

10 Trim the quilt square. If you want to round the corners as I did, use a large dinner plate to mark and then trim the corners with scissors. You will also need to bind the quilt with strips cut on the bias. If you leave the corners square, you can bind with fabric strips cut on the straight of grain.

11 Cut enough 2½" (6.4cm) strips (either straight of grain or bias) in assorted blue fabrics which, when joined, measure at least 280" (711.2cm). Press to make your double-fold binding and then bind your quilt.

12 Add a label to the back of your quilt, perhaps including the words to the rhyme as I did, and cherish for generations!

Ring-A-Roses Table Runner

Make a coordinating table runner by piecing a simple patchwork background using 4" (10.2cm) finished four-patch units and 4" (10.2cm) finished plain squares, then add a selection of appliqué shapes from the quilt using leftover scraps. I've curved the edges of the runner too to match the quilt and bound the whole thing using bias cut strips. My runner measures 16" x 32" (40 x 81.2cm) but can easily be adapted to fit your table ... just add or subtract blocks to get the desired size.

The Forest Farmhouse

in *Autumn*

Projects

The forest sees almost daily changes in colour and light as summer turns to autumn. Leaves turn from green to gold, amber and deep reds before falling on the lanes and paths that crisscross through the trees. The sky has changed, becoming darker, more brooding and intense and this new light brings a unique glow and jewel-like brightness to everything it touches. Find a clearing in the forest, where the trees thin and a plume of smoke rises from the chimney of a farmhouse. The cosy glow from the windows tells you you've arrived at the Forest Farmhouse.

At the Forest Farmhouse the projects are as cosy as the log burner, and reflect the bright and warm colours which surround the house. Clear skies at night and the heavens above are reflected in my Sky Full of Stars Quilt, a scrappy masterpiece that is sure to become a family heirloom. The first frost brings with it almost bare branches and shiny berries, captured in a beautiful appliqué table runner and place settings, which sit alongside a trio of patchwork tie-on cushions, perfect for a cosy meal around the farmhouse table. Stay snug and warm beneath my scrap-busting Little Crosses Quilt, full of the colours of autumn or build your very own cabin hideaway with my Log Cabin in the Woods Quilt.

Cosy *Farmhouse* Style

Cosy farmhouse style takes its inspiration from the land, the farms and the hedgerows. Earthy and rich colours abound with deeply hued walls, rich wooden furniture and a nod to the farming past with old implements given new life – milk churns and vintage kitchenalia, cartwheels and old stone jars. Country crafts are everywhere; wicker baskets, corn dollies and an old spinning wheel decorate the living space and remind its inhabitants of its ancient roots.

Farmhouse colours in autumn reflect the changing landscape: deep fruit colours, plum, damson and cranberry red, chestnut, gold and deep bronze, warm navies and vintage blues, a smattering of bubblegum pink and bright aqua. These colours are deep, dark and rich but also bright and lustrous, just like the berries and autumn leaves in the trees.

I've used lots of reproduction fabrics for the following projects. American Civil War-style fabrics work well and checks, plaids, tone-on-tone and textural fabrics too. I've also used batiks, which have a wonderful deep richness and natural texture, plus some large-scale floral prints and a very clever 'cheater' fabric that imitates Victorian crazy patchwork. Neutrals are warm and rich tans, creams and tea-dyed cottons or rich dark charcoal greys for a quilt with all the drama of an autumn thunderstorm!

Sky Full of Stars Quilt

BEGINNER/
INTERMEDIATE

My Sky Full of Stars Quilt was inspired by my love of the night sky, particularly on a cold and clear autumn night when I can light a fire, wrap up warm and just sit and star-gaze. Stars are one of the oldest motifs in art and a firm favourite of quilters for centuries. I've used my darkest, most intensely coloured scraps for this one and set them against a backdrop of light, bright and warm-toned creams. It's a real showstopper and a quilt you will love making. Take it slowly and enjoy the process. I worked on all the small stars first and searched through my richly coloured and jewel-bright scraps for star points and centres, then dug into my stash of creams, ecru and tan prints for backgrounds. I made more star blocks than I needed. Extras give me options when I put my big blocks together and they mean I don't have to compromise when it comes to balancing the colours. There's no such thing as spare blocks in my home; every scrap gets used and if they don't go into the quilt I'll make pillows, a bag or a Christmas stocking with what's left.

The small stars are teamed with a single chain block which combines assorted cream and tan scraps with deep terracotta red and rust prints to link the stars and blocks together. Use this chain to link the quilt with your decor – if you favour more blues and greys in your home, use those colours in the chain in place of the terracotta. The same scrappy stars will take on a whole new look that coordinates with your home style. The sashings and border are another place where you can adapt this pattern to fit your own taste. Pick out colours and prints that reflect your home rather than trying to reproduce my quilt exactly.

PROJECT SIZE

Finished quilt 86 x 86" (218.4 x 218.4cm)

Block size 24 x 24" (61 x 61cm)

Number of blocks 9

Star block size 6 x 6" (15.2 x 15.2cm)

Number of star blocks 81

Chain block size 3 x 3" (7.6 x 7.6cm)

Number of chain blocks 108

YOU WILL NEED

· Assorted medium and dark prints for the star blocks including some reproduction prints, batiks, tone-on-tones and geometrics. Use as many prints as you can find. You will need the equivalent of eight-one 10 x 10" (25.4 x 25.4cm) squares – smaller scraps are absolutely fine

· Approximately 30 fat quarters or the equivalent in scraps of assorted cream/ecru/tan prints and shirtings for the backgrounds to the stars, the plain blocks and the chain blocks

· Approximately ¾ metre assorted terracotta and rust scraps for the chain blocks

· 1 metre jade green narrow stripe print for the sashings

· 1 fat quarter of dark brown print for the sashing cornerstones

· 1¼ metres large-scale brown stripe print for the border. You will need to join widths together to make the required length, so if your print is very large you may require more fabric to allow for matching patterns

· 91 x 91" (231.1 x 231.1cm) batting

· 91 x 91" (231.1 x 231.1cm) backing fabric

· Thread to piece and quilt

· 1¼ metres binding fabric. I used a second jade narrow stripe print

Continue overleaf...

SKILLS USED

· Precise patchwork
· Making quarter square triangles (QSTs)
· Adding sashings and cornerstones
· Adding a simple border
· Layering and quilting
· Joining strips with diagonal seams
· Binding a quilt

Let's make the quilt!

1 Make the star blocks. From one cream print cut two squares each 3¼ x 3¼" (8.3 x 8.3cm) and from a second cream print cut four 2½ x 2½" (6.4 x 6.4cm) squares. From one dark/medium print cut two squares each 3¼ x 3¼" (8.3 x 8.3cm) for the star points and from a second dark print cut one 2½ x 2½" (6.4 x 6.4cm) square for the star centre.

2 Use the two cream and two medium/dark print 3¼ x 3¼" (8.3 x 8.3cm) squares to make the star point units. Take one cream and one medium/dark print square and pair up, right sides together. Mark both diagonals. Sew ¼" (6mm) on one side of each drawn line, from the outer corner to the centre of the unit, four short seams in total. Cut the unit apart on both diagonals to yield four units. Sew them together in pairs to make two QSTs units. Make two more units with the remaining cream and medium/dark print squares.

3 Arrange the QST units around the centre square and add cream squares at the corners. Sew the units into rows, press the seams in opposite directions and then join the rows. Your star block should measure 6½ x 6½" (16.5 x 16.5cm) at this stage.

4 Make 80 more star blocks, a total of 81 for the quilt. I like to make at least six extras (see project introduction).

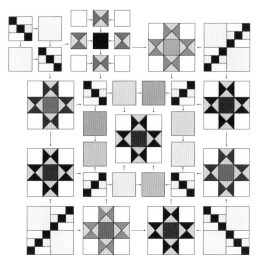

Continue overleaf...

5   Make the chain blocks next. From assorted terracotta and rust prints cut three squares each 1½ x 1½" (3.8 x 3.8cm). From assorted cream/tan prints cut two rectangles each 1½ x 2½" (3.8 x 6.4cm) and two 1½ x 1½" (3.8 x 3.8cm) squares.

6   Arrange the squares and strips as shown overleaf and sew together into three rows. Press the seam allowances towards the rust/terracotta prints. Sew the rows together and press the seams open. Your chain block should measure 3½ x 3½" (8.9 x 8.9cm) at this stage. Make 108 in total.

7   From assorted cream/tan prints cut 144 squares each 3½ x 3½" (8.9 x 8.9cm).

8   Make one large block. This is done using nine star blocks, 12 chain blocks and 16 plain cream print squares. Arrange everything to make the block then sew together into larger units as before: one large centre unit, four corners and four star units. Sew all these units together in three rows and then sew the rows together. Make sure you take care to press the seams in opposite directions and keep the unit joins nicely lined up and accurate as you sew.

9   Press your block. It should measure 24½ x 24½" (62.2 x 62.2cm) at this stage. Make a total of nine large blocks.

10 Cut your jade sashing pieces. You need 24 rectangles of sashing, each 1½ x 24½" (3.8 x 62.2cm). From the dark brown print cut a total of 16 squares, each 1½ x 1½" (3.8 x 3.8cm), for the cornerstones. Arrange the sashings and cornerstones around the blocks then sew the sashing rows and block rows together. Join the rows and press your quilt top. The top should measure 76½ x 76½" (194.3 x 194.3cm) at this stage.

11 Cut your border pieces next. You will need eight strips each 5½" (14cm) wide x width of fabric (42"/106.7cm). Cut off the selvedge and then join the strips in pairs to make pieces that are approximately 86" (218.4cm) in length. From this length cut four border strips, each 5½ x 76½" (14 x 194.3cm) long.

12 From the dark brown print fat quarter, cut four squares each 5½ x 5½" (14 x 14cm) for the border corners.

13 Sew border strips to two opposite sides of the quilt centre and press towards the borders. Sew a 5½ x 5½" (14 x 14cm) square to either end of the remaining border strips and press towards the border fabric. Sew these borders onto the two remaining sides of the quilt and press towards the borders. Your quilt top should now measure 86½ x 86½" (219.7 x 219.7cm).

14 Layer your quilt top with batting and backing fabric. Quilt as desired. I quilted all over with a swirling paisley design.

15 Trim the backing and batting even with the quilt top and then bind your quilt.

16 From your binding fabric cut nine strips each 2½" (6.4cm) x width of fabric and join them end to end with diagonal seams. Use this strip to bind your quilt using the directions on page 45.

17 Add a label, wait until nightfall then look up (or down) and gaze in wonder at the galaxy of stars!

Log Cabin in the Woods Quilt

INTERMEDIATE

When the first winds of autumn start to blow and the leaves begin to fall from the trees, all I want to do is retreat from the cold and into the cosiness and warmth and darkness inside. I've always felt a certain affinity with bears, and at this time of year, I do as they do and think about hibernation! What better place to escape the chill than a log cabin deep in the woods, silent and still and surrounded by the rich hues of falling leaves? My Log Cabin in the Woods Quilt is a scrappy classic taken to new heights with rich dark fabrics set against warm, buttery creams and tans. The piecing is quite straightforward but the whole thing relies on accuracy if everything is to fit together easily. Traditionally a log cabin centre is red, signifying the fire or hearth at the centre of the house. On one side is the light sunlit half of the cabin and on the other are the shadows. Everything is beautifully balanced in this quilt as it is in nature.

PROJECT SIZE

Finished quilt 58 x 58" (147.3 x 147.3cm)

Block size 10 x 10" (25.4 x 25.4cm)

Number of blocks 16

YOU WILL NEED

- At least 20 fat quarters of assorted dark print fabrics and at least 20 fat quarters of assorted light/cream/tan print fabrics for the log cabin blocks and the half square triangle (HST) borders
- Red fabric for the block centres. One 2½" x 42" (6.4 x 106.7cm) strip would be sufficient. I went for a deep rusty red and used four or five different fabrics
- 1½ metres dark large-scale floral for the wide border
- ½ metre cream print for the narrow outer border
- ½ metre deep blue print for the binding.
- 66 x 66" (168 x 168cm) quilt batting
- 66 x 66" (168 x 168cm) backing fabric
- Threads for piecing and quilting

SKILLS USED

- Patchwork
- HSTs
- Adding a border
- Adding a pieced border
- Layering and quilting
- Binding a quilt with a double fold binding

Let's make the quilt!

The fabric quantities may seem like a lot for a quilt of this size but a lot of fabric is hidden in the seam allowances when the pieces are small. I used a lot of layer cake squares alongside fat quarters, scraps and a bit of yardage. The longest strip you will need for your log cabin blocks is 10½" (26.7cm), which of course you can't cut from a 10" x 10" (25.4 x 25.4cm) square – except we are quilters and our superpower is joining fabrics together to make bigger pieces! I often joined smaller pieces of the same fabric in this quilt.

Continue overleaf...

1. I like to do a fair bit of cutting ahead of sewing when I make log cabins. I'll cut lots of strips the size I need but leave them all full length. This is how I recommend making log cabin blocks. It gives me lots of choice when I come to piece the blocks and I can trim each log to size before I sew it to the block. Cut everything to the correct size. This keeps your blocks accurate and if the logs aren't fitting your blocks, it's a sign that your seam allowance is either too big or too small. Take time to make small adjustments and your blocks will be perfect!

2. Cut lots of light/cream/tan strips each 1½" (3.8cm) wide and as long as your piece of fabric. Do the same with the dark prints. Keep the piles separate. I like to start with about 20 strips each of light and dark. As I sew I'll cut four or five more every couple of blocks. Also cut some 2½ x 2½" (6.4 x 6.4cm) red squares for the centre of the block. You'll need 16 in total but you don't have to cut all of them at the start.

3. The log cabin starts from the centre red square and builds outwards from that, one log at a time. I always start with a dark log. Make sure you always work either clockwise or anticlockwise and stick to it!

4. This block is sewn in 'rounds', so let's start with round 1. Start with your 2½ x 2½" (6.4 x 6.4cm) centre square and sew a 1½ x 2½" (3.8 x 6.4cm) strip of dark fabric to one side, pressing the seam allowance away from the centre square. Sew a different 1½ x 3½" (3.8 x 8.9cm) strip of dark fabric to the next adjacent side, pressing the seam allowance away from the centre square. Now sew a 1½ x 3½" (3.8 x 8.9cm) strip of light fabric to the next adjacent side, press the seam allowance away from the centre square and finally sew a different 1½ x 4½" (3.8 x 11.4cm) light strip to the final side of the centre square, pressing the seam away from the centre square. Your block should measure 4½ x 4½" (11.4 x 11.4cm) at this stage.

5. Following the same method as before, sew round two: dark 1½ x 4½" (3.8 x 11.4cm), dark 1½ x 5½" (3.8 x 14cm), light 1½ x 5½" (3.8 x 14cm), light 1½ x 6½" (3.8 x 16.5cm).

6. Round three: dark 1½ x 6½" (3.8 x 16.5cm), dark 1½ x 7½" (3.8 x 19cm), light 1½ x 7½" (3.8 x 19cm), light 1½ x 8½" (3.8 x 21.6cm).

7. Round four: dark 1½ x 8½" (3.8 x 21.6cm), dark 1½ x 9½" (3.8 x 24.1cm), light 1½ x 9½" (3.8 x 24.1cm) and finally light 1½ x 10½" (3.8 x 26.7cm).

8. If you have problems sewing this first block, stop and assess why. If your logs are too long and are hanging over the edge of the block, either you've cut the logs the wrong length or your seam allowance on the previous round was too big. If your logs are falling short of the end of the block then your seam allowances are too small. Please don't trim the logs or block to fit! You're only saving up problems for later and your quilt won't go together (that's when a quilt becomes a UFO – Un-Finished Object).

9. Your block should measure 10½ x 10½" (26.7 x 26.7cm) at this stage. Make a further 15 blocks, 16 in total, and cut more fabrics as you go. Keep plenty of variety in your fabrics!

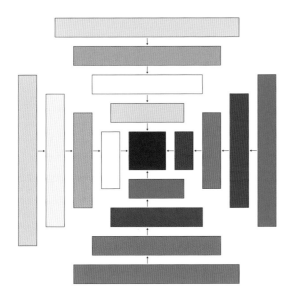

12 Sew 20 HST units together to make a border that is 40½" (102.9cm) long. Make four in total. Press the seams open. Sew one of these borders to two opposite sides of the quilt and press the seam allowances towards the quilt centre. From light scraps cut four squares each 2½ x 2½" (6.4 x 6.4cm) and sew these to either end of the remaining two borders. Sew the last two borders plus corner squares to the remaining two sides of the quilt centre.

13 Add the plain border next. I cut my fabrics on the lengthwise grain so that there were no joins. I have specified enough fabric to do this.

10 Arrange the blocks into four rows of four. This is where the fun really begins. There are lots of different ways you can set 16 log cabin blocks. Have a play, take lots of photos and pick the design which makes you happiest. Sew the 16 blocks together in four rows of four blocks.

11 Make the HST units for both inner and outer borders. From your light scraps cut a total of 92 squares each 2⅞ x 2⅞" (7.3 x 7.3cm). From your dark scraps cut 92 squares each 2⅞ x 2⅞" (7.3 x 7.3cm). Pair a light and a dark square, mark the diagonal on the back with a pencil and sew ¼" (6mm) either side of the marked line. Cut the squares apart on the drawn line and press the seams towards the dark fabric to make two HST units measuring 2½ x 2½" (6.4 x 6.4cm). Repeat to make a total of 184 HST units.

14 From the lengthwise grain of your dark floral print cut two strips each 4½ x 44½" (11.4 x 113cm) and two strips each 4½ x 52½" (11.4 x 133.4cm).

15 Sew the border strips to your quilt, pressing seam allowances towards the wide border.

16 Add your second HST border. Sew 26 HST units together. Make four. Press the seams open.

17 Sew HST borders to two opposite sides of the quilt and press the seams towards the wide border. From light scraps cut four squares each 2½ x 2½" (6.4 x 6.4cm) and sew to either end of the remaining HST borders. Sew these borders to the remaining two sides of the quilt and press. Your quilt should be 56½ x 56½" (143.5 x 143.5cm) at this stage.

Continue overleaf...

18 Add the plain light cream print border. From the cream border fabric cut six strips of fabric each 1½" (3.8cm) x width of fabric (42"/106.7cm) and join the strips end to end. From this strip cut two lengths each 56½" (143.5cm) and two lengths each 58½" (148.6 cm). Sew the last border to the quilt.

19 Layer your quilt top with batting and backing fabric and baste together. Quilt as desired. I used traditional feather quilting. Alternatively you could cross-hatch the light areas and wide border and ditch quilt the dark logs and the HST borders (see note).

20 Trim your batting and backing fabric even with the quilt top.

21 From the dark blue print fabric cut a total of seven strips 2½" (6.4cm) wide x 42"–44" (106.7–111.7cm) long and join with diagonal seams. Press the seams open. Use this strip to bind the quilt using the instructions on page 45.

22 Add a label to your quilt and prepare to snuggle down until the first week of spring!

What is ditch quilting?
Ditch quilting is going through the edge with fewer layers so when hand-sewing it's easier to push through with your needle.

Little Crosses Quilt

Even in the darkest months of autumn, when the flowers are gone and even the berries have been nibbled from the trees, my Little Crosses Quilt will bring radiant colour and joy to your home. This easy quilt uses every scrap to create a thing of beauty and purpose. The main body of the quilt is made up of dark crosses on light backgrounds then around the edge is a 'mock border' of light squares on dark backgrounds. A narrow border helps to frame everything and the final outer border is made from a fabulous 'cheater' cloth I found many years ago and stashed for a rainy autumn day. A cheater cloth imitates patchwork, in this instance Victorian crazy patchwork, and seemed the perfect addition to this quilt. A beautiful rich floral border would work well too, or an extravagant strip, but if you really want to pull out all the stops use my instructions for the Crazy Patchwork Cushion (see page 112). Piece 9" (22.9cm) square blocks then cut in half and piece together a 4½" (11.4cm) border strip to finish your quilt in true Victorian style!

PROJECT SIZE

Finished quilt 75 x 75" (190.5 x 190.5cm)
Block size 5 x 5" (12.7 x 12.7cm)
Number of blocks 86

YOU WILL NEED

- 61x 5 x 5" (12.7 x 12.7cm) charm squares (or equivalent scraps) of medium and dark patterned prints for the dark crosses
- 61x 5 x 8" (12.7 x 20.3cm) pieces of assorted cream and tan prints for the backgrounds of the little crosses blocks in the main body of the quilt
- 60x 5½ x 5½" (14 x 14cm) squares of assorted medium and dark prints for the main body of the quilt
- 24x 5 x 5" (12.7 x 12.7cm) charm squares (or equivalent scraps) of cream and tan prints for the light crosses in the mock border
- 24x 5 x 8" (12.7 x 20.3cm) pieces of assorted dark and medium prints for the backgrounds of the little crosses blocks in the mock border
- 24x 5½ x 5½" (14 x 14cm) squares of cream and tan prints for the mock border
- ½ metre medium jade green plaid for the inner plain border

- 1 metre mock patchwork or patterned fabric for the outer border (you will need to cut widthwise strips and join them; if you don't want joins, allow 2 metres and cut the border strips lengthwise)
- 81 x 81" (205.7 x 205.7cm) quilt batting
- 81 x 81" (205.7 x 205.7cm) quilt backing fabric
- Threads to piece and quilt
- ¾ metre deep red print for the binding

SKILLS USED

- Basic patchwork
- Adding simple borders
- Layering and quilting
- Binding a quilt with double-fold binding

Let's make the quilt!

1   Start by making the quilt centre. This is made up of 61 little crosses blocks with a dark cross on a light background and 60 plain alternate squares, each 5½" x 5½" (14 x 14cm) and cut from medium and dark print fabrics. Cut all 60 alternate squares and set aside.

Continue overleaf...

2 From a medium or dark print, cut one
   1½ x 3½" (3.8 x 8.9cm) strip and two 1½ x 1½"
   (3.8 x 3.8cm) squares. From a 5 x 8"
   (12.7 x 20.3cm) cream or tan print, cut four
   2½ x 2½" (6.4 x 6.4cm) squares and four
   1½ x 1½" (3.8 x 3.8cm) squares.

3 Sew one 1½ x 1½" (3.8 x 3.8cm) light and
   one 1½ x 1½" (3.8 x 3.8cm) dark print square
   together and press the seams towards the
   dark print. Make two.

4 Sew one 1½ x 1½" (3.8 x 3.8cm) light print
   square to either end of the 1½" x 3½" (3.8
   x 8.9cm) dark strip and press the seams
   towards the dark fabric.

5   Arrange the pieced units into rows with the 2½ x 2½" (6.4 x 6.4cm) background squares.

6   Sew the rows together and then join the rows, flipping the seam allowances in opposite directions. Press your block. It should measure 5½ x 5½" (14 x 14cm) at this stage.

7   Make a total of 61 little crosses blocks in this manner with a dark or medium cross on a light background.

8   Lay out your 61 crosses blocks and your 60 medium and dark alternate squares in 11 rows of 11 blocks. You will have six rows of six crosses and five alternate blocks, and five rows of five crosses and six alternate blocks. Use the photographs as a guide. Sew the units into rows and join the rows, pressing the seam allowances in opposite directions throughout. Your quilt centre should measure 55½ x 55½" (141 x 141cm) at this stage.

9   Make the little crosses for the mock border next. Use your 24 light pieces to cut the cross pieces and your dark and medium 5 x 8" (12.7 x 20.3cm) pieces to cut the backgrounds. Piece a total of 24 little crosses blocks with a light cross on a medium or dark background.

10 Arrange the light crosses and light alternate 5½ x 5½" (14 x 14cm) squares around the quilt centre. Sew 11 crosses and squares together to make the side border. Make two and sew them in place, then sew the remaining 13 crosses and squares together to make the top and bottom borders. Sew these in place. Your quilt centre should now measure 65½ x 65½" (166.3 x 166.3cm).

11 From your inner border fabric cut and join seven strips each 1½" (3.8cm) x width of

fabric (42"/106.7cm), then cut the border pieces from this joined strip: two strips each 1½" (3.8cm) x 65½" (166.3cm) and two strips each 1½" (3.8cm) x 67½" (171.5cm). Sew the shorter lengths to the two shorter sides, press back and then sew the two longer strips to the remaining sides and press. Quilt now measures 67½" x 67½" (171.5 x 171.5cm).

12 From your border fabric either cut eight strips each 4½" (11.4cm) x width of fabric and join together, or cut from the length of the fabric two strips each 4½ x 67½" (11.4 x 171.5cm) and two strips each 4½ x 75½" (11.4 x 191.8cm).

13 Sew the side borders on first and press, then add the top and bottom borders and press. Your quilt top is finished and should measure 75½ x 75½" (191.8 x 191.8cm).

14 Layer your quilt top with batting and backing, baste then quilt as desired. I quilted feathers and plumes from edge to edge.

15 Trim and bind with eight strips. Refer to Basic Techniques to finish binding quilt.

16 Add a label to your quilt.

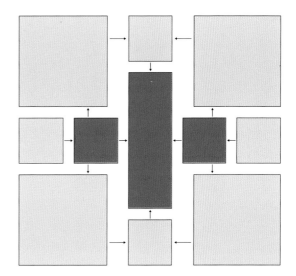

First Frost Table Runner

INTERMEDIATE

My First Frost Table Runner celebrates the beauty of autumn foliage and fruits against an inky background. Autumns can be bleak and dark but the beauty of a few bright berries against a naked branch or fallen leaves on the pavement can lift my spirits like nothing else!

Simple patchwork blocks, sewn in an ombré effect of light to dark, create a dramatic backdrop for the machine appliquéd branches, leaves and berries to pop against. The corners are rounded and the edge bound with bias-cut strips of fabric, but you can leave it square if you prefer.

You can adapt this quilt for any time of the year. For spring, use the smallest flowers from the Ring-A-Roses Quilt (see page 127) with small leaves for cherry blossom on a soft blue ombré background. For summer, use the large flowers and leaves in abundance on an ombré yellow background and for winter use the bare branches, perhaps with just a few really bright berries on a very icy pale background. It really is a versatile pattern!

PROJECT SIZE

Finished runner 45 x 17" (114.3 x 43.1cm)

Block size 4 x 4" (10.2 x 10.2cm)

Number of blocks 38

· See pullout sheet for templates

YOU WILL NEED

· 16 fat eighths ranging from very dark charcoal or black to very light ash/silver grey
· Light and medium green scraps for the leaves
· Plum, rust and peach scraps for the berries
· 1 fat quarter of medium dark brown print for the branches
· 1 fat quarter of black print for the setting triangles
· 1 metre fusible appliqué web
· 21 x 49" (53 x 124.5cm) quilt batting
· 21 x 49" (53 x 124.5cm) backing fabric
· ½ metre fabric for the binding; I used a jade green stripe
· Threads to match your appliqués and for piecing and quilting

SKILLS USED

· Simple patchwork
· Fusible machine appliqué
· On point setting
· Adding setting triangles
· Cutting and using bias-cut binding to finish a quilt

Continue overleaf...

Let's make the runner!

1 Start by making some strip sets. Pick your four darkest background fabrics and cut three strips, 1½ x 21" (3.8 x 53cm), from each.

2 Arrange one of each strip to create a pleasing arrangement and then sew together to make a strip set that measures 4½ x 21" (11.4 x 53cm). Make three strip sets in total. Cut 10 squares from the strip sets, each 4½ x 4½" (11.4 x 11.4cm). You will have a little left over, which can be used to make the matching placemats (see page 158).

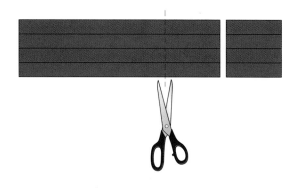

3 Pick four medium dark prints from your remaining background fabrics and repeat steps 1 and 2 to make another 10 blocks.

4 Repeat steps 1 and 2 with your medium background fabrics to make 10 more background blocks.

5 Repeat steps 1 and 2 with your lightest fabrics, but this time you only need two strip sets, from which you will cut a total of eight background blocks.

6 From your fat quarter of black print for the setting triangles, cut a total of five squares, each 7 x 7" (17.8 x 17.8cm). Cut them on both diagonals to yield a total of 20 side setting

triangles. Cut two squares, each 3¾ x 3¾" (9.5 x 9.5cm), and then cut these squares on one diagonal to yield a total of four corner triangles.

7 Arrange your ombre blocks and setting/corner triangles as shown. Sew into diagonal rows and then sew the rows together, pressing the seams in opposite directions.

8 Your background panel should measure approximately 45" x 17" (114.3 x 43.1cm).

9 The fun really starts now – let's do the appliqué! Onto the paper backing of your fusible web, trace one main branch, one medium and three small branches (or a combination of your own) using the templates on the pull out sheet. Trace lots of large medium and small leaves and a mix of large, medium and small berries. Iron your traced shapes onto your chosen fabrics and then cut each shape out neatly on the drawn line. Peel the paper backing off your shapes and arrange them on the pieced background.

10 It's a good idea to start with the large branch and then tuck the medium and smaller pieces under it. Don't fuse anything yet.

11 Arrange the large, medium and small leaves, making sure that they do not extend into the binding area of the runner. Keep a ½" (13mm) minimum margin all around the edges clear.

12 Finally, add the berries in casual groupings. When you're happy with the positions and balance, fuse everything into place with your iron.

13 Stitch around the appliqués using matching threads and a small zigzag or a machine blanket stitch.

14 Layer your runner top with batting and backing and quilt as desired. I used a Baptist fan pattern, which has a smart modern look but is very traditional.

15 Cut and join enough 2½" (6.4cm) strips, cut on the bias to make 110" (279.4cm) of binding, following the instructions on page 45.

16 Label your runner and lay the table with autumn style!

First Frost Placemats

BEGINNER

My First Frost Placemats work beautifully with the table runner of the same name to create a beautiful table for autumn entertaining. They are very adaptable too – and would make perfect place settings for a summer party as well. The curved edges make these a slightly more challenging make using binding cut on the bias. You can leave the corners square and opt for a regular quilt binding if you prefer to keep things simple.

PROJECT SIZE
Finished placemats 13 x 16" (33 x 40cm)
· See pullout sheet for templates

YOU WILL NEED
· 16 small scraps of assorted grey fabrics from very pale smoke through to charcoal, each one 3" x 1½" (7.6 x 3.8cm)
· 5½" x 16½" (14 x 41.9cm) light grey/white print for the upper part of the placemat
· 6½" x 16½" (16.5 x 41.9cm) deep charcoal print for the lower part of the placemat
· Scraps of assorted light green prints for the leaves; plum, copper and peach scraps for the berries; and a rectangle of medium brown batik for the branch, 4" x 12" (10.2 x 30.5cm)
· Small amount of fusible web for appliqué
· 17 x 20" (43.1 x 50.8cm) backing fabric
· 17 x 20" (43.1 x 50.8cm) quilt batting
· 1 fat quarter of fabric for the binding; I used a jade green stripe
· Threads for piecing, quilting and to match your appliqué fabrics

SKILLS USED
· Simple patchwork
· Fusible appliqué
· Layering and quilting
· Cutting and applying bias binding to a quilt

Continue overleaf...

Let's make the placemats!

1 Arrange the 3 x 1½" (7.6 x 3.8cm) rectangles in a pleasing order. I ordered them from light to dark. Sew them together using ¼ inch seam allowance to create a panel 3" (7cm) wide x 16.5" (42cm) in length. Press your seams to one side and then carefully trim the strip to 2½" (6.4cm) wide.

2 Sew the upper and lower portions of the placemat to the top and bottom edges of the pieced strip. Press the seam allowances towards the upper and lower panels. Your panel should measure 13½ x 16½" (34.3 x 41.9cm).

3 Trace large, medium and small leaves onto fusible web, using the photo on page 158 as a guide. Fuse the web to the wrong side of various green scraps and cut out the leaves neatly on the drawn lines. Trace a number of large, medium and small berries onto the fusible web and fuse to assorted plum, copper and peach scraps, then cut out. Finally trace the branch onto fusible web, fuse to medium brown fabric and then cut the branch out neatly.

4 Remove the paper backing from each of the shapes. Scratch a small X on the back of the paper with a pin to help you peel the paper from the shapes and prevent fraying of the edges.

5 Arrange the appliqués onto the background panel. Use my version as a guide but feel free make it your own and add extra stems, leaves and berries.

6 When you're happy with the arrangement of branch, leaves and berries, fuse them in place with a dry iron.

7 Using a small zigzag or a machine blanket stitch and threads that match your appliqués, sew the appliqués in place.

8 Layer your top with batting and backing and baste in place with basting spray or curved safety pins. Quilt as desired. I marked a 1½" (3.8cm) cross-hatch grid using a ruler and a heat-erasable pen, then quilted using a walking foot.

9 Trim the batting and backing even with your quilt top. Use a small saucer or curved object to round off the corners of your placemat. Carefully trim the curved edges.

10 Make approximately 65" (165.1cm) of 2½" (6.4cm) bias-cut binding following the instructions on page 48.

11 Use the folded strip to bind the placemat. Start from the front and then flip the folded edge to the back and either hand sew or pin the binding in place and machine sew from the front 'in the ditch' between the binding and the background of the placemat.

12 Make more placemats, with each one just a little (or a lot) different!

Patchwork Dining Chair Cushions

BEGINNER

My Patchwork Dining Chair Cushions look wonderful tied to a wooden chair seat – the kind of seat that needs some padding to be made comfortable enough to spend hours sitting on, relaxing after a hard day in the garden with a warming casserole and good company! Repurpose extra blocks and units or piece fresh patchwork and add borders or sashings to make them fit your chairs. The ties keep the cushions in place so you can relax. Why not make a set for your kitchen chairs, or take them out into the garden and use them to make wooden garden chairs more comfy?

There are three patterns here and each one will make a 16 x 16" (40 x 40cm) or 18 x 18" (45.7 x 45.7cm) cushion. It's easy to add or subtract units, sashings and borders to increase or decrease the size and make these tie-on cushions fit your farmhouse chairs. I used blocks and units left over from making quilts, but I have given full instructions if you're making these from scratch.

PROJECT SIZE

Finished cushion 16 x 16" (40 x 40cm) or 18" x 18" (45.7 x 45.7cm)

YOU WILL NEED

- Orphan blocks, extra patchwork units or a wide variety of scraps in assorted light, medium and dark prints. See individual cushion instructions for details of colours
- ½ metre coordinating patterned fabric for the backing and the ties
- 20 x 20" (50.8 x 50.8cm) or 22 x 22" (55.9 x 55.9cm) quilt batting
- 20 x 20" (50.8 x 50.8cm) or 22 x 22" (55.9 x 55.9cm) plain cotton to back the cushion top
- Threads for piecing and quilting
- 16 x 16" (40 x 40cm) or 18 x 18" (45.7 x 45.7cm) cushion pad (pillow form)
- Small square up ruler (optional)

SKILLS USED

- Patchwork
- Adding sashings
- Adding borders
- Layering and quilting
- Making an envelope backing
- Making ties

Continue overleaf...

Rail Fence Cushion

You'll need a wide assortment of medium and dark prints in rich autumnal tones such as chestnut, brown, deep russet, turquoise, deep blue, black and purple, or colours to tone with your decor. Each scrap needn't no more than 1½" x 4½" (3.8 x 11.4cm) but if you have longer strips you can speed up construction. You might have leftover units from the First Frost Table Runner (see page 154) needing a good home!

1   Cut four strips each 1½ x 4½" (3.8 x 11.4cm) in a variety of dark prints. Sew them together side by side and press the seams one way to make one rail fence unit 4½ x 4½" (11.4 x 11.4cm). If your scraps allow, cut strips 1½ x 10" (3.8 x 25.4cm) or multiples of 5" (12.7cm) long. Sew four of these strips together, press then cut into 4½" (11.4cm) units. You'll have this cushion made in no time!

2   Make a total of 16 rail fence units.

3   Arrange the units into four rows of four units, alternating the direction of the strips in each unit to create a woven effect.

4   Sew the units into four rows and press the seams in alternate directions.

5   Sew the rows together and press the whole cushion front. This will make a 16" x 16" (40 x 40cm) cushion pad. You could layer, quilt and finish the cushion now or add a border in the next step.

6   To create a border, add two 1½ x 16½" (3.8 x 41.9cm) strips to opposite sides of the cushion front, press towards the border then add 1½" (3.8cm) x 18½" (47cm) strips to the remaining two sides to create an 18 x 18" (45.7 x 45.7cm) finished cushion pad. If you want it to be 20 x 20" (50.8 x 50.8cm), add 2½" (6.4cm) strips to all sides. You get the idea!

7   Follow the finishing instructions on page 169 to complete your chair cushion.

Half Square Triangle Cushion

You'll need a wide variety of light, cream and tan prints and lots of medium and dark prints for this project. You might have left over half square triangle (HST) units from your Log Cabin in the Woods Quilt project (see page 144), too. I've added a slender light border followed by a wider dark border.

1 From your light scraps cut a total of 18 squares each 3 x 3" (7.6 x 7.6cm). Cut 18 squares of the same size from your medium or dark fabrics.

2 Pair up a light and a dark square and mark the diagonal lightly in pencil on the back of the light square. Sew ¼" (6mm) either side of this marked line.

3 Cut the square on the marked line to yield two HST units. Use a small square up ruler to trim your units to 2½ x 2½" (6.4 x 6.4cm).

4 Make a total of 36 HST units, each 2½ x 2½" (6.4 x 6.4cm).

5 Now the real fun begins! Arrange and rearrange your units in a 6 x 6 grid until you have a pattern that pleases you. Sew the units together in rows, press the seams in opposite directions and then sew the rows together. Your cushion centre should measure 12½ x 12½" (31.7 x 31.7cm) at this stage.

6 Add 1½ x 12½" (3.8 x 31.7cm) strips of cream print to two opposite sides and press, then add 1½ x 14½" (3.8 x 37.8cm) strips to the remaining two sides to make the centre 14½ x 14½" (37.8 x 37.8cm) square. Adding another border the same width will make a 16 x 16" (40 x 40cm) finished cushion. If you want an 18" x 18" (45.7 x 45.7cm) finished cushion pad, add 2½" x 14½" (6.4 x 37.8cm) strips of dark print to opposite sides and press then add 2½" x 18½" (6.4 x 47cm) strips to the remaining two sides.

7 If you don't have enough of one fabric to cut all four sides, take a mix and match approach. Use 'lookalikes' or four completely different fabrics. This is totally in keeping with country style quilting and will give your project real charm and authenticity!

8 Follow the finishing instructions on page 169 to complete your chair cushion.

Little Patchwork Crosses Cushion

You'll need a variety of medium and dark grey prints for the block backgrounds and small scraps of various aqua and teal prints for the crosses. You'll also need a fat quarter of deep rust-gold for the sashings and border and some fabric for the backing and ties. I used some extra units from my Little Crosses Quilt (see page 151) to create my cushion. The quilt goes beautifully with this cushion and would look lovely as a table cover.

1 From one medium/dark grey background print cut four squares each 2½ x 2½" (6.4 x 6.4cm) and four squares each 1½ x 1½" (3.8 x 3.8cm). From one teal or turquoise print cut two squares each 1½ x 1½" (3.8 x 3.8cm) and one strip 1½ x 3½" (3.8 x 8.9cm).

2 Sew a teal and grey small square together and press the seam towards the grey print. Make two. Sew a small grey square to either end of the 1½ x 3½" (3.8 x 8.9cm) teal strip and press the seams towards the grey squares.

3 Sew a 2½" (6.4cm) grey square to either side of the grey/teal square unit. Press the seams towards the large squares. Make two.

4 Arrange the pieced units and sew the three strips together. Your patchwork unit should measure 5½ x 5½" (14 x 14cm) at this stage.

5 Make a total of nine little crosses blocks. Arrange your blocks in three rows of three.

6 From your deep rust-gold sashing fabric cut six strips each 1 x 5½" (2.5 x 14cm). Sew these sashing strips to join the little crosses blocks into three vertical columns.

7 Cut two strips of sashing each 1" x 16½" (2.5 x 41.9cm) from the deep rust-gold print and sew between the columns of blocks to join them together. Your cushion front should measure 16½" x 16½" (41.9 x 41.9cm) at this stage.

8 Cut two border strips each 1½ x 16½" (3.8 x 41.9cm) and sew them to opposite sides of the cushion front. Press the seam allowances towards the border strips.

9 Cut two strips of border fabric 1½ x 18½" (3.8 x 47cm) and sew them to the remaining sides of the cushion front, which should now measure 18½ x 18½" (47 x 47cm).

10 Follow the finishing instructions overleaf to complete your chair cushion.

Finishing instructions for all cushions

1   Layer your cushion front with batting and backing fabric (a solid cotton fabric is perfect) and quilt the top. It's best to quilt these cushions quilt densely to make them sturdy and strong, as you'll be sitting on them. Once quilted, trim the batting and backing even with the quilt top.

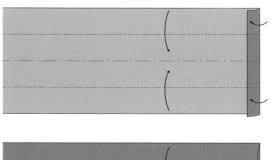

2   Make the ties next. Cut four strips of fabric each 4 x 21" (10.2 x 53cm). Fold a ½" (13mm) hem on one short end and press, then fold, the strip in half lengthwise. Press, then open out and fold the outer raw edges in to meet the centre fold and press again. Finally refold the strip down the centre fold to create a neat 1 x 20½" (2.5 x 52cm) tie. Topstitch ⅛" (3mm) in from each of the long edges. Make four.

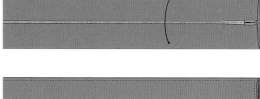

3 Position a tie 1½" (3.8cm) down from the back corner, placing the raw edge of the tie level with the raw edge of the cushion front, and baste in place. Repeat with another tie 1½" (3.8cm) down from the adjacent side. Repeat this on the other back corner with the remaining two ties. Carefully pin the ties to the centre of the cushion front to keep them out of the way as you make up the cushion.

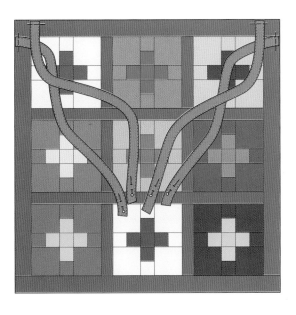

4 Make an envelope backing for the cushion. Cut two panels, either 16½ x 12" (41.9 x 30.5cm) or 18½ x 14" (47 x 35.6cm) depending on the size of your cushion front. Fold and sew a double ½" (13mm) hem on the inner edge of each panel, then layer them onto the front of your cushion. Pin in place then sew with a ¼" (6mm) seam allowance all around the outside edge.

5 As these cushion covers are likely to need regular laundering it's a good idea to overlock or finish the raw edges of the cushion with a wide zigzag stitch.

6 Turn the cushion through to the right side and unpin the ties. Insert your cushion pad and plump before tying onto your chair.

7 Kettle on. Sit back. Relax!

Christmas in the country

Projects

Wherever you find yourself at Christmas time, be it on the coast, or a market town, a farmhouse in a forest or even in the city centre, surely every one's heart is at least a little bit in the country. I have spent many Christmases in a great many locations and I have always made the best of wherever I found myself. But I always want to recreate a little bit of country charm, bring in a sense of those long-ago traditions that ground these holidays in family and in past times. Quilts are the perfect way to make anywhere feel like home so, even when I'm staying with friends or in hotels, I'll take a quilt along for the ride and bring a little festive country charm with me.

There's nowhere I'd rather celebrate this happy season than the countryside, surrounded by friends, in a home decorated with a festive wreath, foraged pinecones and evergreens. Tones of red and white provide a festive contrast – a combination beloved by quilt makers too. The Christmas tree, whether humble or huge, is decorated with its branches decorated with tiny candles, glass baubles and a scattering of Embroidered Tree Decorations. Warm yourself by a roaring fire, hung with a selection of my Times Past Christmas Stockings, patiently waiting for St Nicholas to fill them. Thrown across the back of a generously padded settee is a quilt that's brought out annually to welcome in the season – perhaps my Star Light, Star Bright design perhaps or the Christmas Beauty. Admire the Christmas on the Lake quilt which covers the bed. It's an elegant red and white classic quilt that will endure, like so many Christmas traditions, for generations.

Grand Country *House* Style

Country house style is all about heirlooms and, if you don't have any, then fake them or make them! A collection of ginger jars displayed on an elegant side table – the product of a distant family member's travels or a shop around the internet? An tasteful chaise, draped with a beautiful quilt, chandeliers, family portraits...

For sophisticated decorating at Christmas I don't think anything looks finer than swags of real evergreens– such as ivy, fir and pinecones dotted with red berries, clementines and bunches of cinnamon sticks tied with red ribbon. All this green needs some contrast so for the perfect marriage I've gone with red and green, a Christmas and quilters classic combination. Don't limit yourself to traditional festive reds, use every tone in the paintbox, from the softest blush pink through to apple blossom, candy and bubblegum to cranberry, holly berry and vivid ruby.

The best part of using every possible permutation of a colour, apart from the visual spectacle, is that you can't really get it wrong. No colour or design is in such large amounts that it's individual presence really matters ... its part of one huge orchestra of colours playing sweetly together!

Country house fabrics include classics such as chintz and wood block printed florals, toile de Jouy and plaids. Look out for large extravagant border prints and pastoral toiles, as mixed with regular quilting fabrics they will bring country house style to your projects. Mix these special fabrics with small geometrics, reproduction-style shirtings and simple homespun cloths for a touch of 'make do and mend.' Thrifting was never an alien concept, even in the grandest of houses, so don't be afraid to mix your fabrics and bring some of the charm of the Red House to your home in winter.

Christmas at the Lake Quilt

ADVANCED

My Christmas at the Lake Quilt is based on a Lady of the Lake quilt block. It's a real classic and traditionally pieced in just two fabrics, often red and white but sometimes blue, yellow or green. For this very special seasonal version I have chosen a huge selection of red, cranberry and pink prints with a mixture of white, cream and tans. The block itself is made from one large half square triangle (HST) surrounded by 20 more small triangle units. It's the kind of block that requires time and patience and a degree of precision but, as always, I have tips and tricks to get you there! I couldn't stop at piecing the blocks so I made pieced sashing and pieced cornerstones too. Even the border is mitred. It's a more advanced technique but it only takes a little time and effort (and the right fabric) and brings rich rewards. The border fabric was in my stash for about 10 years. I found it on sale in a quilt shop and I knew it would be perfect for a quilt one day. The border design was printed vertically so I could cut it on the lengthwise grain, meaning that the side borders are seamless. I have given instructions for cutting your fabric in the same way. If you use a non-linear print for the border you could cut it in widthwise strips and piece the border, which will use less fabric. This is a quilt to take your time over. Make it slowly and enjoy every stitch!

PROJECT SIZE

Finished quilt 85 x 85" (215.9 x 215.9cm)

Block size 9 x 9" (22.9 x 22.9cm)

Number of blocks 25

Pieced sashing 3 x 9" (7.6 x 22.9cm)

Number of pieced sashing units 64

Pieced cornerstones 3 x 3" (7.6 x 7.6cm)

Number of cornerstones 40

YOU WILL NEED

- At least 20 fat quarters of red/cranberry/ pink prints or the equivalent in fat eighths, yardage or scraps for the blocks and pieced sashing/cornerstones
- At least 20 fat quarters of cream/tan/ white prints for the blocks, sashings and cornerstones
- 1¼ metres white-on-white print for the setting triangles
- 3 metres of fabric if the design is printed with a vertical pattern which you want to use without joining strips. Otherwise, 2 metres of fabric is sufficient but you will need to join strips together (see project introduction)
- 91 x 91" (231.1 x 231.1cm) backing fabric
- 91 x 91" (231.1 x 231.1cm) quilt batting
- ¾ metre fabric for binding
- Spray starch
- Small square up ruler
- Threads for piecing and quilting

SKILLS USED

- Precise patchwork
- Pieced sashing and cornerstones
- 'On point' setting
- Adding a mitred border
- Layering and quilting
- Adding a double-fold binding

Continue overleaf...

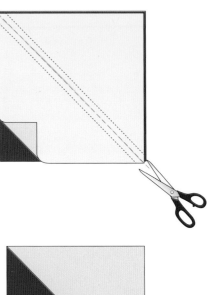

Let's make the quilt!

Use a ¼" (6mm) seam allowance throughout but be prepared to make it a little scant if you find your units coming out smaller than they should.

1 Start by making one Lady of the Lake block.

2 Choose one red/pink print and one white/tan/cream print to work with on this block. Give both fabrics a light spritz with spray starch and press well to firm the fabric up a little.

3 From both prints cut one 6⅞ x 6⅞" (17.5 x 17.5cm) square and ten 2⅜ x 2⅜" (6 x 6cm) squares. Layer the two large squares right sides together and mark the diagonal lightly in pencil. Sew ¼" (6mm) either side of this line and then cut along on the drawn diagonal. Press the seams towards the red/pink fabric. This makes two half square triangle (HST) units, which should measure 6½ x 6½" (16.5 x 16.5cm) raw edge to raw edge. Set one HST unit aside to use in another block.

4 Pair one red/pink and one white/tan square, right sides together, and cut on the diagonal. Sew these triangle pairs together and press towards the darker fabric. Repeat with the remaining 2⅜ x 2⅜" (6 x 6cm) squares to make a total of 20 HST units, which should measure 2 x 2" (5 x 5cm) raw edge to raw edge.

5 Arrange one large HST and the 20 small HSTs to make the block. Make sure you get the light and dark sides of the triangles in the correct orientation. Sew four HST units together and press the seams open. Repeat. Sew these units either side of the large HST unit. Press the seams open. Sew six HST units together, repeat and press the seams open. Sew these units to the remaining two sides of the block and press the seams open.

Continue overleaf...

6 Measure your first block at this stage to ensure correct sizing.

7 Make a further 24 blocks (25 in total).

8 Make the sashing next. Cut 128 strips of cream/tan/white fabrics, each 1½ x 9½" (3.8 x 24.1cm). Cut 64 strips of assorted red/cranberry/pink prints, each 1½ x 9½" (3.8 x 24.1cm)

9 Arrange one cream/tan or white strip either side of a red/pink one. Sew the strips together and then press towards the darker fabric. Your unit should measure 3½ x 9½" (8.9 x 24.1cm) raw edge to raw edge. Make a total of 64 pieced sashing units. You can strip piece (see page 25) these units to speed things up. Cut strips of cream 20" (50.8cm) long or in multiples of 10" (25.4cm). Do the same with the red/pink. Sew them together in threes and press, then cut 9½" (24.1cm) segments from this unit. If you have any leftovers you might be able to use some of them in the cornerstones.

10 Make the cornerstones next. You need to make a total of 40 cornerstone units, which are little nine-patch blocks. Each cornerstone has five red/pink squares and four cream/tan white squares, each 1½ x 1½" (3.8 x 3.8cm). You could cut and sew individual squares together – I did make some of the cornerstones like this. Cutting and piecing individual units is the very best way to make sure you use every little scrap, but it takes longer! For a lot of the cornerstones I cut lengths of red/pink and white/tan/cream strips, each 1½" (3.8cm) wide by however long a scrap I had. I pieced three of them together, two pink or reds and a white, or two tan/cream and one red/pink. You need twice as many 2 x red and 1 x cream units, so keep that in mind as you're cutting and piecing. Press seams towards the red/pink fabrics throughout and then cut 1½" (3.8cm) segments from your strip pieced units. Finally put three units together as shown and sew. Check that your units measure 3½ x 3½" (8.9 x 8.9cm) at this stage.

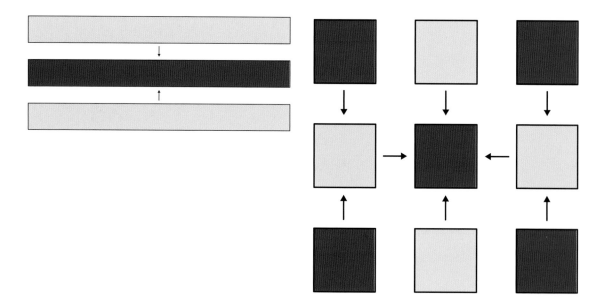

11 This quilt features the blocks set on point, which means we must cut 'setting triangles' and 'corner triangles' to square the whole thing up. These triangles are cut in such a way that the edge of your quilt will be on the straight of grain – stable, not stretchy, and easy to add a border to. I've done the maths. You've got this! From your white print fabric cut three squares each 18¼ x 18¼" (46.3 x 46.3cm), then cut these squares on both diagonals to yield a total of 12 side triangles. From the remaining white fabric cut two squares each 11½ x 11½" (29.2 x 29.2cm) and then cut them on one diagonal to yield a total of four corner triangles.

12 Set out your blocks, sashings and pieced cornerstones as shown. Take pictures and check your photos. You will spot a block turned the wrong way up or a block that isn't working in a photograph in a way that you just don't in real life.

13 Sew the setting triangles, corner triangles, blocks, sashings and cornerstones together in diagonal rows. Your centre should measure approximately 72 x 72" (183 x 183cm) square.

14 From your border print fabric cut four identical border strips each 6½ x 90" (16.5cm x 228.6cm). This is a little longer than you need but you will find the extra length a bit of security! My border print had 6½" (16.5cm) wide repeats on it so I added a ½" (13mm) seam allowance and cut strips that were 7" (17.8cm) wide. I only did this because of the print I was using. Do the same if you wish – you might just find the perfect print!

15 Find the centre of each strip and mark it with a pin. Pin each border strip to the four sides of your quilt, starting and stopping pinning ¼" (6mm) in from the raw edge of your quilt top. Let the excess hang off each end. Sew the strips to the four sides of the quilt top, starting and finishing ¼" (6mm) in from the raw edge.

16 Mitre the first corner. Fold the quilt top in half at the corner, on the diagonal so that the border strips line up and sit on top of each other. Use your long rotary cutting ruler to draw a line on the border fabric, in line with the fold on your quilt top. Mark this line with pencil. Pin it well and then sew the line, starting from the very corner of your quilt top and sewing out to the edge. Open the border fabrics. Check the accuracy of your mitre and if you are happy with it, trim the excess fabric from the border pieces leaving a ¼" (6mm) seam allowance. Press the mitred seam open. Repeat on the remaining three corners.

A

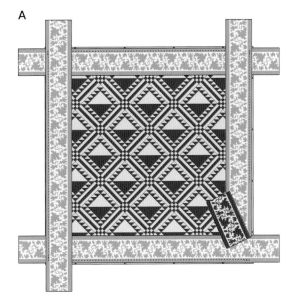

Continue overleaf...

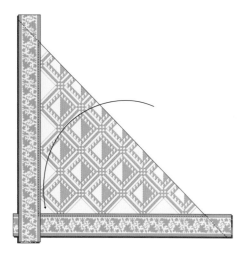

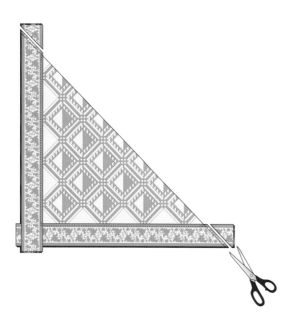

17 Press your quilt top and then layer it with backing and batting. Quilt as desired. I chose a swirling design of pomegranate-like fruits and leaves. I do love a pomegranate at Christmas!

18 Trim the backing and batting even with the quilt top. From your binding fabric cut nine strips each 2½" (6.4cm) x width of fabric and sew them together using diagonal seams. Press the seams open.

19 Bind the quilt using the double-fold method (see page 45).

20 Add a label to the reverse of the quilt and pour yourself a little festive drink – whatever the time of year! Merry Christmas!

Star Light, Star Bright Quilt

BEGINNER/
INTERMEDIATE

My Star Light, Star Bright Quilt is sure to become a part of your Christmas celebrations. Imagine waking up under it on Christmas morning! The combination of rich and deep holly berry reds and soft creams is vibrant and classic but the scrappy background prints and smart 'square on point' border bring this quilt right up to date. This quilt would look so good in any combination of cream/tan background and one-colour scraps for the stars and borders, or why not use the colours in the Sky Full of Stars Quilt (see page 138) or the quilts in The Dower House in Summer (see pages 100 and 106) to inspire a multicolour version. You'll make this quilt more than once, I'm sure!

PROJECT SIZE

Finished quilt 72 x 72" (183 x 183cm)

Block size 16 x 16" (40 x 40cm)

Number of blocks 9

YOU WILL NEED

· At least 16 fat quarters (or equivalent in meterage or scraps) assorted cranberry and holly berry red prints for the blocks and pieced border

· At least 16 fat quarters (or equivalent in meterage or scraps) of assorted light cream prints for the blocks and pieced border

· 1 metre cream print for the inner border

· 1 metre deep red stripe print for the outer border

· ¾ metre deep red print for the binding

· 78 x 78" (198.1 x 198.1cm) quilt batting

· 78 x 78" (198.1 x 198.1cm) quilt backing fabric

· Thread to piece and quilt

SKILLS USED

· Patchwork piecing

· Adding borders

· Adding pieced borders

· Layering and quilting

· Adding a double-fold binding

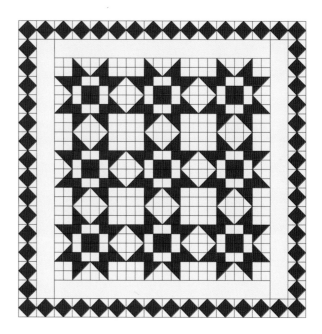

Continue overleaf...

Let's make the quilt!

1   To make the block centre, cut four squares each 2½ x 2½" (6.4 x 6.4cm) and sew them together to make a four-patch. From assorted cream fabrics, cut four rectangles each 2½ x 4½" (6.4 x 11.4cm) and from assorted red prints cut four squares each 2½ x 2½" (6.4 x 6.4cm). Arrange the four-patch, rectangles and squares as shown and sew together.

2   From assorted red prints cut a total of four squares each 4⅞ x 4⅞" (12.4 x 12.4cm) and cut each one once on the diagonal to yield a total of 16 triangles. Reserve eight of them for another block. From assorted cream prints cut eight squares each 2½ x 2½" (6.4 x 6.4cm) and set aside. Also cut eight squares each 2⅞ x 2⅞" (7.3 x 7.3cm) and cut these squares once on the diagonal to yield a total of 16 triangles.

3   Arrange two small cream triangles and one cream square as shown and sew together. Press the seams towards the triangles. Make eight. Sew one cream triangle/square unit to a large red triangle and press the seams towards the red triangle. Make eight. Sew two red/cream triangle units together to make a large pieced flying geese unit.

4   Cut 16 squares each 2½ x 2½" (6.4 x 6.4cm) from assorted cream prints and sew together in groups of four. Make four x four-patch units in this way for the block corners.

5   Arrange the block centre, the large flying geese units and the four-patch corner units as shown and sew together to make one large Star Bright block, which should measure 16½ x 16½" (41.9 x 41.9cm) at this stage. Make a total of nine blocks.

6   Arrange the nine Star Bright blocks into three rows of three blocks and sew them together. Press the seams in opposite directions. Your quilt centre should measure 48½ x 48½" (123.2 x 123.2cm).

7   From the cream inner border fabric cut six strips each 4½" (11.4cm) x width of fabric and sew end to end. From this strip cut two border strips each 48½" (123.2cm) long and two border strips each 56½" (143.5cm) long. Sew the first border to the quilt following general instructions for add a plain border. You quilt should now measure 56½" x 56½" (143.5 x 143.5cm).

8   Make the Square in a Square units next. From your assorted red prints cut a total of 60 squares each 3⅜ x 3⅜" (8.6 x 8.6cm). From assorted cream prints cut a total of 120 squares each 2⅞ x 2⅞" (7.3 x 7.3cm) and cross-cut these squares on one diagonal to yield a total of 240 triangles.

Some quilt patterns have a certain magic when four blocks come together and create a brand new extra design or secondary pattern. Star light, star bright is a great example of this.

9   Arrange four assorted cream triangles around a red square and sew triangles to two opposite sides. Press the seam allowances towards the triangles. Sew the remaining two triangles to the last two sides. You unit should measure 4½ x 4½" (11.4 x 11.4cm). Make a total of 60 Square in a Square units.

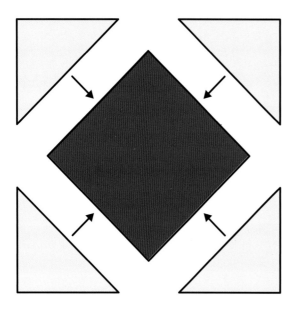

10 Sew the Square in a Square units together in rows of 14 and press the seam allowances open. Make four borders in this way.

11 Sew borders to two opposite sides of the quilt and press the seams towards the inner cream border. Sew the last four Square in a Square units to either end of the last two border strips and then add these border strips to the quilt. Your quilt should now measure 64½ x 64½" (163.8 x 163.8cm).

12 From your dark red border fabric cut seven strips each 4½" (11.4cm) x width of fabric and sew them together. From this strip cut four border strips each 4½ x 64½" (11.4cm x 163.8cm). From assorted red prints cut four squares each 4½ x 4½" (11.4 x 11.4cm) for the outer border corners.

13 Sew two of the border strips to opposite sides of the quilt. Press the seams towards the plain border. Sew the corner units to either end of the remaining two border strips and sew these borders to the last two sides of the quilt. You quilt should measure 72½ x 72½" (184.1 x 184.1cm).

14 Layer your quilt top with batting and backing and baste. Quilt as desired. I quilted mine with large paisley-style plumes for a rich and opulent look.

15 Trim your batting and backing even with the quilt top.

16 From your binding fabric cut a total of seven strips each 2½" (6.4cm) x width of fabric and join with diagonal seams. Use this strip to bind the quilt.

17 Add a label.

18 Look forward to the night before Christmas … you are so ready!

Christmas Beauty Quilt

My Christmas Beauty is the perfect lap-sized quilt to snuggle under, throw on the back of a sofa for instant winter decorating or hang on the wall behind a bed. The quilt is based on a Blackford's Beauty quilt, which I have made much easier to piece with modern stitch-and-flip techniques. It takes just four big blocks plus borders to make this beauty, so you'll have it whipped up in time for mulled wine on Christmas Eve.

I've been inspired by the beauty of old French textiles and country-house fabrics for this quilt. I used a combination of deep madder red, soft slate blue and grey and lots of tan. Mixing larger French-style florals, reminiscent of Indian wood-block and chintz fabrics, with smaller ditsy prints and geometrics creates an elegant quilt, perfect for bringing country-house style to your home.

Even grand ladies in country houses had to economise sometimes and so as a nod their thrift I have used two different 'lookalike' prints for the outer border. It's something often seen in vintage quilts – even very fine ones!

PROJECT SIZE
Finished quilt 50½ x 50½" (128.2 x 128.2cm)
Block size 18 x 18 (45.7 x 45.7cm)
Number of blocks 4

YOU WILL NEED
· 1 metre warm cream print for the block backgrounds
· ½ metre lighter cream print for the stitch-and-flip units
· ½ metre solid caramel or tone-on-tone print for the star points
· 4 fat quarters of assorted madder reds for the block construction and for the sashing cornerstones
· 4 fat quarters of assorted slate blue prints for the blocks
· 2 fat quarters of red/slate blue large-scale floral prints for the block centres and outer border corners
· ½ metre tan/red/slate blue floral for the sashings

· Two ½ metres of 'lookalike' slate blue floral prints or 1 metre of a single print for the outer border
· 56½ x 56½" (143.5 x 143.5cm) backing fabric
· 56½ x 56½" (143.5 x 143.5cm) quilt batting
· ½ metre binding fabric in small red/tan geometric print
· Threads to piece and quilt

SKILLS USED
· Simple patchwork
· Stitch-and-flip patchwork
· Adding sashings
· Adding simple borders with cornerstones
· Layering and quilting
· Joining strips with a diagonal seam
· Binding a quilt

Continue overleaf...

Let's make the quilt!

The following instructions are to make one block.

1 Each Blackford's Beauty block is 18 x 18" (45.7 x 45.7cm) finished and is made of nine units each 6½" x 6½" (16.5 x 16.5cm).

2 Make the block's corner units first. From assorted madder red prints cut four squares each 2 x 2" (5 x 5cm), then from background cream/tan fabric cut two strips each 2 x 5" (5 x 12.7cm), two strips each 2 x 3½" (5 x 8.9cm) and two squares each 2 x 2" (5 x 5cm).

3 Sew a 2 x 2" (5 x 5cm) square of red to one end of a 5" (12.7cm) strip and press the seam towards the red fabric. Make two. Sew a cream/tan 2 x 2" (5 x 5cm) square to an assorted red 2 x 2" (5 x 5cm) square and press towards the red fabric. Sew the red square to a 3½" (8.9cm) strip of cream/tan, again pressing the seams towards the red fabric. Make two.

4 Arrange the four strip units to make the block as shown. Sew the rows together and press the seams open. Your unit should measure 6½ x 6½" (16.5 x 16.5cm) at this stage. Make another three units per block, four in total.

5 Make the four star point units next. From a slate blue print fabric cut two rectangles each 3½ x 6½" (8.9 x 16.5cm). From your lighter cream/tan print cut two squares each 3½ x 3½" (8.9 x 8.9cm) and from the solid caramel cut two squares each 3½ x 3½" (8.9 x 8.9cm).

6 On the back of both cream/tan squares and both solid caramel squares mark the diagonal from corner to corner lightly with a sharp pencil. Layer one light cream/tan square onto the top edge of your slate blue rectangle, diagonal drawn line as shown. Pin then sew directly on this line. Flip the corner of the cream square back and press. Check the fit! It should perfectly cover the fabric underneath it with no gaps or overhang. If it isn't to your liking, unpick and have another go. If you're happy with the results, fold the corner back to its original position, trim the underlying fabric to ¼" (6mm) seam allowance and press again.

7 Repeat the stitch-and-flip process on the same rectangle with a solid caramel square, positioning it at the bottom of the rectangle this time, with the diagonal line running in the same direction. Stitch, flip, check and then trim.

Continue overleaf...

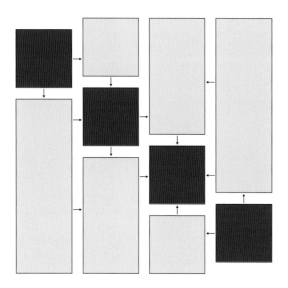

8 Make a second stitch-and-flip unit as before, but this time you want the direction of the diagonal drawn line running in the opposite direction.

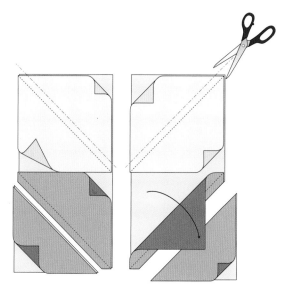

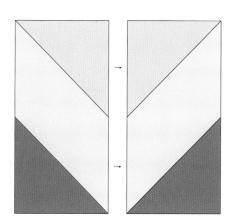

9 Sew the two rectangular stitch-and-flip units together and press the seam open. Your unit should measure 6½ x 6½" (16.5 x 16.5cm) at this stage. Make four units in total using the same fabric combination.

10 From large-scale madder red/slate blue print cut one 6½ x 6½" (16.5 x 16.5cm) centre square.

11 Arrange the nine units to create the block. Sew the blocks into three rows of three units and press the top and bottom rows away from the centre unit and the middle row, with the seams pressed towards the centre square. Sew the rows together.

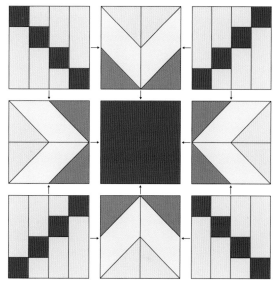

12 Your block should measure 18½ x 18½" (47 x 47cm) at this stage.

13 Make four blocks in total if you want to make a wall hanging, using a different slate blue print in each block and a couple of different prints for the centre units for variety. (Just for the record, one block on its own makes a super cushion.) Nine blocks make a beautiful large throw and 12 or 20 blocks will make a 3 x 4 or a 4 x 5 arrangement – perfect for either a single or double bed quilt.

Continue overleaf...

14 From your tan/slate blue/red floral print cut the sashing. You will need 12 pieces each 2 (5cm) x 18½" (47cm). From the small red/tan geometric print cut nine cornerstone squares, each 2 x 2" (5 x 5cm).

15 Arrange the four blocks in two rows of two, with the sashings and cornerstones set around the blocks. Sew the block rows together and the sashing rows between them, then sew the rows together. Your quilt centre should measure 41" x 41" (104.1 x 104.1cm) at this stage.

16 From each of your two border prints cut two strips each 5½" (14cm) x 41" (104.1cm) (four in total) and from your two centre unit fabrics cut two 5½ x 5½" (14 x 14cm) squares (four in total) for the outer border corners.

17 Sew the borders to the top and bottom edges of your quilt centre. Press the seams towards the border.

18 Sew one of each 5½ x 5½" (14 x 14cm) squares to either end of the remaining two border strips and sew these borders to the quilt centre. Press the seams towards the border strips. Your quilt should now measure 52 x 52" (132 x 132cm).

19 Layer your quilt top with batting and backing fabric. Quilt as desired. I chose to quilt an edge-to-edge design of fruis and leaves which for me gives a nod to the bounty of Christmas without being too specific.

20 Trim the batting and backing even with the quilt top.

21 Cut six strips of binding fabric, each 2½" (6.4cm) x width of fabric (42"/106.7cm) and join end to end with diagonal seams. Press the seams open then press the strip in half lengthwise, wrong sides together. Use this strip to bind your quilt.

22 Add a label and celebrate the beauty of Christmas and quilting!

Times Past Christmas Stockings

My Times Past Christmas Stockings were inspired by the tradition of using old quilts for something else. Once it had become so worn, faded and threadbare that it couldn't be used on the bed any more, an old quilt would find new purpose, perhaps as the filling for another quilt. It might be cut up and used to make a winter jacket or cushions. Here 'quilt fragments' are used to make decadent and beautiful Christmas stockings.

I have recreated the look with newly made patchwork and quilting, but if you have an old and worn quilt that you want to repurpose, jump straight to cutting out the stockings. I've made this stocking with half square triangles and with mini nine-patch blocks, but you could experiment with other small patchwork, too.

PROJECT SIZE
Finished stocking 20 x 13" (50.8 x 33cm)
· See pullout sheet for templates

YOU WILL NEED
· Assorted scraps of red and pink prints, including a couple of larger scraps for the toe and heel appliqués
· Assorted scraps of cream and tan prints, including a few larger pieces for the embroidered pennants
· 1 fat quarter of cream print for the bias binding
· 1 fat quarter of cream print for the backing
· ½ metre plain cream fabric for the stocking lining
· 3 large and 3 small red buttons
· 22" x 30" (55.9 x 76.2cm) quilt batting
· Threads for piecing, appliqué and quilting
· Embroidery floss in cranberry red (or I used a cranberry red) and a crewel needle
· Template material

SKILLS USED
· Using templates
· Simple patchwork
· Making quarter square triangles (QSTs)
· Interfaced appliqué
· Hand embroidery
· Layering and quilting
· Sewing buttons
· Making bias binding
· Making a tie

Let's make the stockings!

1   For the quarter square triangle (QST) version I made a total of approximately 65 x 2" (5cm) finished QST units, using 3¼" (8.3cm) squares of cream and pink/red fabrics paired together and following the instructions for making simple patchwork on page 25.

2   For the nine-patch version of the stocking I made approximately 14 nine-patch blocks using five 1½ x 1½" (3.8 x 3.8cm) squares of red/pink prints and four 1½ x 1½" (3.8 x 3.8cm) squares of cream prints sewn together. I also cut approximately 15 x 3½" x 3½" (8.9 x 8.9cm) plain squares of assorted cream prints and sewed the nine-patch blocks and the plain squares together.

Continue overleaf...

3 Use your own orphan patchwork units or even sew 2½" (6.4cm) squares of assorted scraps together to make enough fabric to cover the stocking template generously. Don't skimp here. You need at least 1" (2.5cm) extra fabric on all sides of the template to allow for shrinkage as you quilt and for seam allowances. At this point of constructing your stocking front, decide the direction you want your stocking to face.

4 Layer your pieced stocking front with a piece of quilt batting and plain cotton lining cut 1" (2.5cm) bigger on all sides. Baste the three layers together and quilt as desired. I quilted the QST version with a Baptist fan design and the nine-patch stocking was quilted with a square grid. Use the stocking template to mark and then trim the patchwork, batting and lining even with the marked stocking.

5 Use the toe and heel appliqué templates to cut one outer and one lining fabric of each. Make sure you orientate the appliqués to fit your stocking depending on whether it is right or left facing. Place an outer and a lining piece right sides together and sew along the marked sides with a short machine stitch. Clip any curves, turn to the right side and press. Position the toe and heel onto the quilted stocking front and baste, then machine stitch the appliqués in place with a double row of stitching.

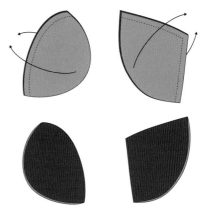

6 Layer your fat quarter of backing fabric with batting and lining fabric and quilt as desired, then cut out a reversed stocking to create the back.

7 If you are making pennants for the top of your stocking, use the template to mark three pennants on your chosen cream fabrics but do not cut them out. Layer the marked fabric with a piece of lining fabric and sew along the marked edges, leaving the top open for turning. Cut the pennants out leaving a scant ¼" (6mm) seam allowance on all sides. Turn through to the right side and press. Use two strands of embroidery floss to work a running stitch along the side edges.

Continue overleaf...

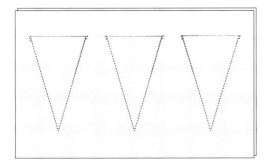

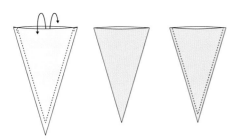

9 From binding fabric cut two strips each 2½ x 12" (6.4 x 30.5cm) and fold in half along the length, wrong sides together, to create straight grain binding. Make two. Use these strips to bind the top edges of the stocking front and the stocking back.

8 Position and then baste the pennants in place along the top edge of the stocking front.

10 Layer the stocking front and back together, linings touching and right sides on the outside. Baste the stocking front and back together ⅛" (3mm) in from the raw edges.

11 From the remaining binding fabric cut 2½" (6.4cm) strips on the bias and sew end to end to make a binding strip approximately 60" (152.4cm) long. Fold and press your binding and use it to bind the side edges of the stocking. Fold the raw edge of the binding over the top edge by ½" (13mm) before you sew to the front stocking then, when you flip the binding to the back, the top will be neat. Hand or machine sew the binding to the reverse of the stocking.

Continue overleaf...

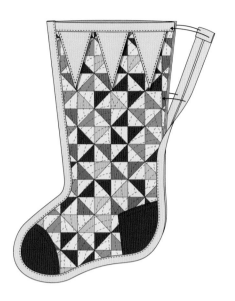

12 Cut a 3 x 16" (7.6 x 40cm) strip of cream fabric for the hanging tie. Fold the strip down the centre, wrong sides together, and press. Open out then fold the raw edges into the centre fold and press again. Finally, re-fold the strip down the centre fold to encase the raw edges and press. Fold and neaten both short ends of the tie and then topstitch on all sides. Fold the tie in half and hand stitch securely to the top of the stocking. Sew a couple of stacked buttons over the join.

13 Sew stacked buttons to the top of each pennant if desired. I use double embroidery floss and leave a long tail on the top side of the button, stitch it in place and then leave a long tail on the top. Tie both tails together in a double knot then trim to leave a little decorative knot on the top of the button.

14 Hang your stockings with care on the mantelpiece!

Embroidered Tree Decorations

INTERMEDIATE

I love making things for Christmas – but I'm a realist too! I like little projects that stand alone or can be added to each year. My Embroidered Tree Decorations also look fantastic pegged to a length of ribbon and strung across a window. You can personalise them quite easily with initials or a date. I dug into my family button tin for mine. For true country style, choose tiny plaid fabrics, a homely ric rac trim and and ready-made sisal tassels that are made for paper crafting. The sisal string I used was from the potting shed!

PROJECT SIZE

Finished decorations 4½" (11.4cm) or 5" (12.7cm)

· See page 206-207 for templates

YOU WILL NEED

· 6 x 6" (15.2 x 15.2cm) white or cream solid fabric
· 6 x 12" (15.2 x 30.5cm) light fusible woven interfacing
· Red embroidery floss and needle
· 12–15" (30.5–38.1cm) red ric rac
· 6 x 13" (15.2 x 33cm) red print fabric
· Decorative button
· 9" (22.9cm) sisal string or fine ribbon
· 1 small sisal tassel
· Small quantity fibrefill or toy stuffing
· Glue stick
· Small wooden embroidery hoop (optional)

SKILLS USED

· Hand embroidery
· Faced appliqué
· Attaching buttons
· Making a pieced backing
· Closing a gap using a ladder stitch

Let's make the tree decorations!

1   Trace one of the snowflake designs onto your piece of white background fabric. It's easy to reduce or enlarge the design so it's a perfect fit. Each snowflake sits inside a corresponding circle. Don't mark or embroider that yet – you'll use it later for marking your backing.

2   Cut a 6 x 6" (15.2 x 15.2cm) piece of interfacing and iron to the wrong side of the background fabric.

3   Hoop the fabric if you wish, then work the snowflake design using a backstitch throughout and French knots for any dots (see page 51).

4   Trace the circle from your chosen snowflake onto the remaining 6" x 6" (15.2 x 15.2cm) interfacing and then lay this on top of your

Continue overleaf...

embroidery. Carefully sew around the circle, sewing directly on the drawn line and using a slightly smaller than normal stitch.

5   Cut a slit in the back of the interfacing and turn the embroidery through to the right side. Push the circular edge out very neatly and then iron in place to fuse the embroidery to the backing.

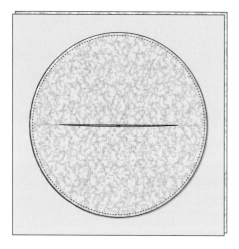

6   Use the glue stick to attach a piece of ric rac around the embroidery edge, tucking half the ric rac under the circle to create a wavy edge. The raw ends need to be tucked under neatly, but this is where you will sew a button so it doesn't have to be perfect! Baste your sisal tassel to the bottom of your embroidery.

7   Use a circle larger than your embroidery to cut out one piece of red print fabric. Pin your embroidery to the centre of this circle and topstitch the embroidery in place, sewing very close to the inner circle edge.

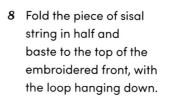

8   Fold the piece of sisal string in half and baste to the top of the embroidered front, with the loop hanging down.

9   Take the rest of the red print fabric and fold it in half, press, then cut through the fold to yield two rectangles. Sew the rectangles together again, leaving a 3" (7.6cm) gap in the centre (see page below). Layer this pieced backing with the embroidered front, right sides together, making sure that the loop and tassel are carefully tucked inside. Sew around the circle using a ¼" (6mm) seam allowance. Trim the backing fabric to within ¼" (6mm) of the seam and turn through to the right side. Press carefully.

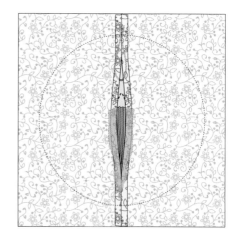

10 Push a little stuffing or fibrefill inside the decoration to pad it out. Slip stitch the opening closed using small hand stitches.

11 Sew your button in place using small hand stitches.

12 Deck the halls!

If you prefer you can use backing fabric instead of interfacing to face the embroidery, following the method on page 50. Turn through and press, close the gap, and carefully glue then topstitch ric rac around the outer edge. Add a button or two for extra country charm!

Suppliers and useful resources

The Quilters' Guild of the British Isles

www.quiltersguild.org.uk
An educational charity that seeks to preserve the heritage of quilting and work to ensure a vibrant future for the craft.

Sewing Street TV

Freeview channel 73, Sky channel 670 or watch online at
www.sewingstreet.com

Sewing machines, fabrics, thread, batting, cutting equipment and rulers

The Bramble Patch
www.bramblepatchonline.com

The Cotton Patch
www.cottonpatch.co.uk

Doughty's
www.doughtysonline.co.uk

Empress Mills
www.empressmills.co.uk

Greenhill Patchwork and Quilting
www.greenhillpatchwork.co.uk

Gutermann thread
www.consumer.guetermann.com

Juki Sewing Machines
www.jukiuk.com

Lady Sew and Sew
www.ladysewandsew.co.uk

The Sewing Studio
www.thesewingstudio.co.uk

Village Fabrics
www.villagefabrics.co.uk

Longarm quilting supplies and longarm quilters for hire

Handi Quilter
Longarm quilting machines, threads and supplies
www.pinholequilting.co.uk

Longarm quilting services

The Bramble Patch
www.bramblepatchonline.com

Farrcorner Quilting
www.farrcornerquilting.co.uk

Greenhill Quilting Services
www.greenhillpatchwork.co.uk

The Quilt Cabin
www.thequiltcabin.co.uk

Haberdashery

Boyes
Fantastic suppliers of notions, batting, fabric, cushion pads, tools and interfacing
www.boyes.co.uk

Dunelm
Cushion pads and general haberdashery
www.dunelm.com

Hobbycraft
General sewing and craft supplies
www.hobbycraft.co.uk

John Lewis
General haberdashery, thread, template plastic, fabric and cutting equipment
www.johnlewis.com

Love Crafts
Quilting fabrics, a huge range of pre-cuts, solids and notions
www.lovecrafts.com

Vlieseline
Fusible web, interfacings and batting/wadding
www.vlieseline.com

Huge thanks to...

Huge thanks to my wonderful husband Charlie...who is unfailing in his support and positive encouragement of all my creative endeavours... you are my greatest ally and my best friend...you always make me feel like I can do anything at all! Huge thanks also to my agents, Heather Holden-Brown and Elly James who are both a constant source of wisdom, calmness and friendship...to Stephanie Milner, Alice Kennedy-Owen, Kuo Chen, Lily Wilson – fabulous locations – and Shamar Gunning and the rest of the wonderful editorial team at Pavilion...where do I start? My name is on the jacket but every one of you puts heart and soul into the books we create together and I am very grateful for the dedication, imagination and hard work by every one of you. Thanks also to Rachel Whiting for once again bringing my ideas to life in the most glorious photography...you breathe life into the quilts I make and every photograph is a thing of beauty. Thank you to everyone at Sewing Street TV who encouraged me along the way but in particular to Hayley M who cleared my diary when I needed to just sit and sew...and who made sure I had all the glorious fabric, waddings and thread I needed to make beautiful things... you're a star! Thanks to Sarah and Mike Noble at Green Cottage, as well as all at the Middleton Lodge Estate for providing the beautiful settings for these projects.

Special thanks to The Quilters Guild of the British Isles who made me patron of their wonderful organisation...thank you for that...but also heartfelt gratitude to you as an organisation and to all the volunteers who work so tirelessly to curate and preserve our quilting past and work so hard to promote quilting to this and future generations.

Lastly, very special thanks to the treasured friends who helped me with making some of the projects in this book... to Joan Drake, dearest friend, confidante and "Deputy", to Rebecca Harrison and Bernadette Owens-Wainwright for taking my Haori to new heights and Lynne Goldsworthy for her amazing sewing skills, all the laughs and more, Chris and Susan Terry for brilliant quilt label making and to Hilary Kancidrowski for her splendid embroidery skills and warm encouragement... and to all the many friends in quilting who support and encourage me in my work...thank you!

Embroidery Templates

How to use: trace the desired shape carefully onto the matt side of freezer/tracing paper. Use a ruler for straight edges and make sure the template you are tracing has the ¼" (6mm) seam allowance added. (All the piecing templates in this book do, but appliqué shapes are always shown without a seam allowance.)

Cut the paper template out carefully with scissors.

See pullout sheet in envelope at the back of the book for all other templates and additional embroidery.

Pavilion
An imprint of HarperCollins*Publishers* Ltd
1 London Bridge Street
London SE1 9GF

www.harpercollins.co.uk

HarperCollins*Publishers*
Macken House
39/40 Mayor Street Upper
Dublin 1
D01 C9W8
Ireland

10 9 8 7 6 5 4 3 2 1

First published in Great Britain by Pavilion
An imprint of HarperCollins*Publishers* 2024

Copyright © Pavilion 2024
Text © Stuart Hillard 2024

Stuart Hillard asserts the moral right to be identified
as the author of this work. A catalogue record of this
book is available from the British Library.

ISBN 978-0-00-858475-7

This book contains FSC™ certified paper and
other controlled sources to ensure responsible
forest management.

For more information visit: www.harpercollins.co.uk/green

Publishing Director: Stephanie Milner
Editor: Clare Double
Editorial Assistant: Shamar Gunning
Design Manager: Laura Russell
Senior Designer: Alice Kennedy-Owen
Designer: Lily Wilson
Artworker: James Boast
Production Controller: Grace O'Bryne
Photographer: Rachel Whiting
Illustrator: Kuo Kang Chen
Proof-reader: Molly Price

Printed and bound by RR Donnelley in China

All rights reserved. No part of this publication may be
reproduced, stored in a retrieval system, or transmitted,
in any form or by any means, electronic, mechanical,
photocopying, recording or otherwise, without the prior
written permission of the publishers.

This book is sold subject to the condition that it shall not,
by way of trade or otherwise, be lent, re-sold, hired out or
otherwise circulated without the publisher's prior consent
in any form of binding or cover other than which it is
published and without a similar condition including this
condition being imposed on the subsequent purchaser.